# Success Stories

Trudy's process has resulted in my making the decision to change the direction of my career. The information she shared caused me to pause, think, reflect, and embrace that which I knew was already in me. I am eternally grateful for having gone through her process. My life is richer. I am happier and I know that I will be more successful in the future.

—Felicia Mooty

I give special thanks to you, Trudy, for helping me to see the beauty on the western horizon. Once my brand was clearly defined, I became more purposeful about my future. I now recognize that sunsets are essential for some incredible moonlit nights and pave the way for the new beginnings of tomorrow. Your process helped me to understand and embrace the power of personal branding! —Julie Washington

Trudy, thank you for your willingness to share. You really changed my life with your insight and knowledge. Defining what my brand is was so enlightening. I never considered how (or that I needed) to set myself apart and now you have given me the information to make it happen. I am excited about the future. You empowered my success. —Reneé Moore

After going through your process I have clarity on my personal life vision. And I now know exactly where my professional objectives fit into that life vision. I always thought that if I worked hard enough the reward would come. What an eye-opening experience to gain respect for the values of sponsors and mentors. I feel like you have been my mentor in my personal career development. Your program encouraged me to stretch in both my personal and professional life to achieve balance and harmony. I am excited about my leadership role and I am on fire about being in charge of my own professional destination. —Virginia Morris

Engaging with you through your process has allowed me to erupt as an individual and renew aspirations which have been dormant within my soul. You have shown me how to reach beyond the target and create new thresholds. Thanks for helping me to fulfill my dreams. —Donna Howard

I am a more effective and stronger leader as a result of going through this program. Anyone who is serious about career advancement will benefit from your work. I have a greater sense of confidence and belief in my ability to produce results. Developing the ability to conceptualize and communicate the business synergies and best practices that I have created positioned me for my recent promotion. I am a believer in the importance of marketing your results. Thank you for opening the door to my future success! —Linda Hennen

I wish that this kind of program had been available when I first began my career. It would have cut my learning curve by many years. I now realize, understand, and embrace my personal responsibility for my career success. What a great process you have designed. Every woman who is serious about career success should have the benefit of this knowledge. —Kimberly Woodard

Trudy is an exceptional person with an exceptional message. In her book, Her Corner Office, she speaks from the heart and personal experience in order to help pave the way for other women to be truly successful in their personal and professional lives. Her "talk to the hand" exercise brought a smile to my face and was a creative spin on how to evaluate decisions.

—Debra J. Gawrych, bestselling author of *The 7 Aspects of Sisterhood: Empowering Women Through Self-Discovery*

# HER
## Corner Office

# HER CORNER OFFICE

A GUIDE TO HELP WOMEN FIND A PLACE AND A VOICE IN CORPORATE AMERICA

TRUDY BOURGEOIS

BROWN BOOKS PUBLISHING GROUP
DALLAS, TEXAS

HER CORNER OFFICE



Manufactured in the United States of America.

For information, please contact:
Brown Books Publishing Group
16200 North Dallas Parkway, Suite 170
Dallas, Texas 75248
www.brownbooks.com
972-381-0009

ISBN 0-9744597-1-2
LCCN 2003114836
2 3 4 5 6 7 8 9 10

*This book is dedicated to all the women who faced and overcame the challenge of honoring their desire to experience personal and professional success. Thank you for your willingness to pave the way for dreams to come true.*

# Contents

# Acknowledgments

To my grandparents, David and Mary Stallworth and Jerome and Arzhelle Reid, who were seed sowers and laid a great foundation. They made the sacrifices that paved the way for my success. To my parents, Clovis and Gerdiest Reid, who sacrificed to give me the education that opened the door to a world of opportunities. To my clients, whom I have had the pleasure and honor of working with and watching grow. To my brothers and sisters, friends, and extended family who encouraged me to share my message with as many people as possible. To my mother-in-law, Normal Bourgeois, who taught me to create my own happiness and success. To Laura Gloege, who worked magic with the whole editing process. To my children, Adam and MaryEllen, who understood when Mommy was at work yet again. To my wonderful husband, Michael, my soul mate, who was with me during all the battles and victories. He was steadfast during my climb to break the glass ceiling. Thank you!

# Introduction

*"Think not of yourself as the architect of your career, but as the sculptor. Expect to have to do a lot of hard hammering and chiseling and scraping and polishing."*

—Author Unknown

I began my professional career almost twenty years ago. When I started I knew only one thing: I wanted to be a leader and make lots of money. I didn't have a clue as to how to go about becoming this professional person. But I knew that my drive to succeed was so strong that I was willing to learn. And learn I did! I read everything possible on career development. I sought to learn everything that I could about being an effective leader. Unfortunately, there wasn't a lot of information about women and careers, let alone minority women and career development. In fact, only a handful of women had been able to penetrate the corporate world in the way that I wanted to, and most of them weren't able to sustain their success. The information that was available about leadership was rooted in a masculine, military, top-down philosophy.

In the beginning I thought that if I worked hard I would get my just reward. How naïve! Please don't misunderstand my message; hard work is extremely important. In fact, "jacks to get in the game" is achieving consistent results. But it takes so much more!

The choice to pursue a career in leadership is extremely serious and should not be taken lightly. You must want to become a true leader in order to build the kind of career that enables you to make a lasting impact. Careers are important, but there is more to life than a career. There's more to you than a job! So clearly understand that designing a career is not a road map for your life success. You must take the time to decide for yourself how a career fits into your whole life.

Once you've made the decision to optimize your professional side, then you need a plan of action. That's what this book offers. Your leadership development is a critical component of this plan.

In order to be successful in today's competitive marketplace, you must take control and responsibility for developing and executing your own personal career strategy. Of course you can't do it alone. It's really no fun to even try to do it alone. It is important as you design your career that you reach out to others. Serving others will be the source of your energy.

The objective of this book is to provide you with direction, guidance, exercises, and strategies that will enhance your career success. This book is not a replacement for career counseling. Neither is it a cookie-cutter approach to developing a successful career.

Success should be defined for yourself. What I define as success may not fit your definition. Career success for the next generation will hopefully not be built in the same way that I experienced it. When I was coming up the ranks, there was no work/life balance. In fact, you couldn't even talk about your kids at the office.

When I was up for my first "real" promotion to the position of district sales manager, I had to be interviewed by the area vice president. He was a good person. In fact, many years later he became my peer. But I can clearly remember him asking me about my family plans. I had shared with him that my husband and I had two kids. He wanted to know if there were going to be any more forthcoming. He was rather relieved when I told him that the baby factory had been relocated to heaven.

He was very professional about his inquiries, but I got his message: "You can't have this promotion and children too." A successful career shouldn't have to be at the expense of your life, your family, or your personal aspirations. I know that's easier said than done, believe me! But I am convinced that it CAN be done.

This book is peppered with ideas of my own, as well as those of others, on ways for you to create the kind of business environment that thrives because of the value that is placed on people. I have done this with the hope that I can sow seeds that will grow within you to give you the strength and resolve to get to the top, remain there, and make a lasting difference!

It is my pleasure to share with you what I know about climbing the corporate ladder. My sincere hope and prayer is that you will use your achievements not to experience success but to experience significance. By being significant, you, too, become a seed sower and lay the foundation to make it easier for generations to come.

I believe that if you take responsibility for your own

career and develop your leadership skills based upon the behaviors and values that are outlined in this book, you can experience professional success at any level.

I have written this book based upon my personal experience and beliefs. I have included case studies that validate my principles and philosophies. The cases are based upon real-life situations. The names have been changed to protect the innocent or the guilty.

"You can bring a horse to water, but you can't make him drink." The same is true with the information that you will get from this book. It is yours to have, but you must act on it. Information in and of itself is not powerful. It becomes powerful when you make the choice to act on it!

Don't try to complete every exercise in the same day. This might sound funny to you, but I know many people who would do just that. Take the time to enjoy this self-discovery. Perhaps this will be the first time that you have seriously taken a look at your career. Or perhaps you have reached a point of disillusionment and need to reposition yourself. Regardless of where you find yourself, start from where you are. And be truthful about the good, the bad, and the ugly. We can only make progress if we dare to look inside.

I wish I could tell you that there is a shortcut. I can't and there isn't. Hard work truly does pay off. And while there are no guarantees in life, I can promise you that if you take the time to invest in yourself by applying the principles found in this book, you will experience success!

## Getting the Most Out of This Book

1. Buy a journal or get a notebook and dedicate it as the place where you will keep your notes.

2. Make yourself stop after every chapter to reflect on what you've learned or what you need to learn in order to accomplish growth in each of the stages.
3. Complete every exercise.
4. Solicit the help of a professional coach or a good friend who can help you stay focused and on track.

## Making the Transformation

Participate in my monthly teleclasses focused on reinforcing the behaviors that will be needed in the career of your dreams! Register to receive information on teleclasses and to receive the monthly e-zine at www.hybridleader.com.

It is my hope that the information contained in this book will help make your career planning process easier and more successful. It is also my prayer that you develop as a transformation leader who will make a tremendous impact on the world. I have given you what I wish had been available to me when I was climbing the corporate ladder. One of my values is making a difference for others. I heard someone say that each of us should want our lives to count. I definitely want my life to count, and I want to help you make your life count as well.

# To Thine Own Self Be True

*"What lies behind us and what lies before us are small matters compared to what lies within us."*

—Ralph Waldo Emerson

## The Fabric of Your Belief System

The nucleus of that which is you is found in your beliefs and values. Belief, as defined by Webster, is a feeling of conviction. Values, on the other hand, are things that are important to you. All of us have well-developed beliefs and values. These deeply rooted philosophies are the sum of the experiences and learning that we have had in life thus far. Our personal beliefs and values serve as the guide for who we currently are and who we will become. To be honest, I didn't realize how strong an influence my own beliefs and values were until I began preparing for an intense coaching session for myself.

A brilliant woman by the name of Juannel Teague conducted the coaching session. My preparation for the session included an assessment of my life's experiences that had served to formulate my beliefs and values. The process was extremely intensive but immensely illuminating. It gave me an opportunity to gain a very deep understanding of the experiences in my life that drove me both personally and professionally. During the course of this process, I discovered many things about myself that I didn't previously have awareness or appreciation for. If you willingly engage in this process, I promise that you, too, will discover things about yourself that you never knew.

It was during the course of this coaching session that I found the courage to take a far more powerful stance on sharing my feelings about climbing the corporate ladder. You might think, "Oh, I already know what my beliefs and values are. I can skip this part." Resist the temptation to do so. Getting your foundation right is critical; understanding the root of your belief and value system is the core of a solid foundation to build a successful career.

The exercises in this book will help you to get in touch with your true beliefs and values. I did these same exercises myself. I promise they work! Like a lot of other people, I was unaware how much the experiences from my childhood were impacting the way I conducted myself as an adult. I think we all know that we are products of our environment, but I don't think we have consciously gathered the wisdom that comes as a result of these experiences.

> [ . . . I believe in the power of making a difference in someone's life. ]

I remember being eight or nine years old, playing in the field next to our house one day. It was a beautiful spring day and Easter was coming. Jackie, a friend who was my age and lived around the corner, came over to play. I thought we were really poor, but he was even poorer than we were.

I probably should mention that there were ten kids in my family. That day, many of my sisters and brothers were outside playing. We were all talking about how excited we were about the upcoming Easter egg hunt. I noticed that Jackie didn't seem to share in our excitement. I remember asking him what was wrong. He told me that his parents couldn't afford an Easter basket and that they were not going to have an Easter egg hunt. I was crushed. It was an emotional experience that I can still feel today. I ran into the house, got my basket, and gave it to Jackie. It was my way of taking away his pain.

[ ...each of us can and should make a positive difference for others. ]

Do you know what I learned from that experience? I learned that I want to help people. I learned that I believe in the power of making a difference in someone's life. That experience formed the nucleus for the kind of leader that I would become. As I progressed in my corporate climb, I realized that the most satisfying part of my job was helping others develop themselves. Today, Jackie is doing great in life. I saw him a few years ago in my hometown and we had a big laugh about how I cried and gave him my Easter basket. He still remembers it as well as I do. If you don't think that there is power in connecting with and touching another person's life, you aren't alive. This experience formulated one of my core beliefs, that each of us can and should make a positive difference for others. It also set the stage for one of my strongest values—helping others realize their dreams. That Easter basket incident was the spark for what I do today professionally. That's how strong and impactful the early experiences are in your life.

## Keeping Your Values Alive

Getting in touch with what you believe and value will be critical to building a career that fits into your life and is rewarding. I now know how much I value my family. I wish I could tell you that I always knew the true value of my family, but the truth is that I haven't always made choices with my family's value at the core. In fact, the value that I place on my family life is what ultimately caused me to make the decision to leave corporate America.

I also value my health. Believe me when I say that without your health you are nothing! If you don't manage the pressure and stress while making your journey, you will pay a price. I paid a price. Have you ever had chest pain and dismissed it as stress? Don't ignore pain! It is a warning sign. I didn't have a heart attack, but I was riddled with anxiety attacks that would sometimes paralyze me. I didn't appreciate the need to manage my energy. Looking back, I wish I had done some things differently, which is part of the reason that I decided to write this book. I hope that by sharing some of the good and bad things that happened to me, your dreams will come quicker and without as high a price. That's why it is so important to understand your beliefs and values. Once they are defined, you can set the boundaries for all aspects of your life so that you know where your thresholds are.

One of my clients recently had an experience that tested

her resolve for her values. She was pregnant with her third child. She had been working toward a promotion for the last several years. She had done a really good job establishing her brand (I'll explain more about the branding concept later). She thought that she was close to being promoted. However, she had been experiencing complications with her pregnancy. Doctors had instructed her to take it easy. She had had problems in the past with her job, and these problems caused her concern about the perception her colleagues might have of her. The problems that she had weren't bad—it was just that the learning curve was so steep that it was taking her longer than she wanted to progress. She really wanted to be viewed as the star employee. She was absolutely torn. She wanted to be visible for the promotion; however, the culture of the company, although progressing, was still not openly understanding of women and pregnancy. At least that's what she thought. The truth is, the company would have responded to the parameters that she asked for. The company would have gladly accommodated each request that enabled her to take care of her health. No company wants an employee to have her baby on the cafeteria floor. Trust me!

Sometimes we are afraid to suggest or admit that we need help or special accommodations, for fear that it makes us look weak. Don't give in to this self-imposed guilt. If my client takes care of herself, then she's more likely to have a healthy baby—and still be considered for the promotion. If she doesn't take care of herself, she puts herself and her child at risk. Although she may still be considered for the promotion, if she makes this choice, she will likely regret it.

Fortunately, my client's situation was resolved through coaching. She was able to come to terms with taking several days off, as her doctor had instructed. She actually found that she was able to get more done lying in the bed than running up and down the halls of the office tower. And, more importantly, she was true to her own values and she demonstrated her beliefs through her actions.

Many people start out their careers with really clear value systems, and then, to "fit in," they compromise their values. Don't do it! Stick with what you know to be right. Use the area below to compose a personal list of values you want to instill in your business environment. Some examples might be excellence, education, or open communication.

______________________________________________

______________________________________________

______________________________________________

______________________________________________

______________________________________________

If you are not able to live your values in the work environment, what is holding you back?

______________________________________________

______________________________________________

______________________________________________

______________________________________________

______________________________________________

What behavioral changes and/or environmental changes do you need to make in order to be able to function with value integrity?

______________________________________________

______________________________________________

______________________________________________

______________________________________________

______________________________________________

> [ If you don't take the time to find out where you stand, you will be compromised. ]

Your beliefs and values represent who you are. Don't let any individual or company serve as a source of compromise in this area. If you don't take the time to find out where you stand, you will be compromised. I promise you that. You are responsible for you! So, what do you believe? What do you value? Stop right now and challenge yourself to see if you can describe your values and beliefs. Then take it to the next level and ask yourself how these values and beliefs have shaped who you are today.

Following are lists of my beliefs and values, which I have refined over the past several years.

I believe . . .

- What you sow, you will reap.
- You should treat others the way you want to be treated.
- You should dedicate yourself to excellence.
- We all have a purpose in life.
- When you help others, you help yourself.
- God does not sleep.
- We should strive to make a positive difference for ourselves and others.

I value . . .

- Spirituality
- Family
- Friends

- Fun
- Honesty
- Trust
- Life
- Productivity
- Learning
- Helping/Caring

I want to encourage you to develop lists for yourself. I also recommend that you keep these lists close at hand as you develop your career plan. Let your personal values and belief system guide your every action.

Let me drive this point home even further. In 1992, I was promoted by my company to the position of area vice president of sales for the southeast region. This region included nine states and approximately eight hundred people. Our team was responsible for a little more than a third of what was then a $6-billion company. It was a great job. In fact, at the time, it was my dream job. I loved interfacing with the customers. I relished the opportunity to create a culture that mirrored my beliefs and values. I created all kinds of new business applications and received lots of press throughout the organization. The whole experience was absolutely invigorating.

There was only one problem. Of course, that one problem was a huge problem. My husband, Mike, was forced to work in another city because the market in which we lived was too small for his television production profession. The kids were spending more time with sitters than with either Mike or me. While managing a travel schedule that kept me on the road for a minimum of three days a week, and after being faced with a cancer scare, I knew that something had to change. But what that truly meant, I didn't know.

[ You have to value yourself before others will value you. ]

After much counsel with my husband, and prayer, I made the decision to approach my boss. I wanted to test the waters on the company's position about a possible relocation to another job. I would have been satisfied with just a kind ear. Unfortunately, I didn't receive that from my boss. But I didn't stop there. There are some battles that are just worth fighting, particularly when they are attached to a strong belief or value. I decided to wage a campaign. The message of the campaign was this: *I want to work here and do great things for this company, but I can't under these circumstances. I've got to find another way. Will someone help me find another way?*

If you are reading this, thinking "I could never do that," think again. You can! Someone has to be the first. You have to value yourself before others will value you. And if you are not willing to help your organization meet your needs, shame on you. *Don't sit on the sidelines; get in the game!*

My colleagues and my boss really thought I was out of my mind to ask the company to relocate me and to create a job for me. Fortunately for me, the chairman and CEO of the company was familiar with my work and the contributions I had made. After I submitted several business plans to the senior vice president and the president, my company and I came to the decision that there was, indeed, a business need I could help to fill. The need was rooted in addressing the company's underdeveloped relationships, performance, and market share within the national accounts. It was a big challenge, but I was glad to take it on in order to move my family to one city where we could all live together. I knew I would still have to travel, but it was a better situation overall. We picked Dallas. It worked for the company since the world's largest convenience store chain was headquartered in Dallas, and the world's largest distributor was less than a two-hour drive from there.

Initially, the situation had seemed hopeless. Had I not asked or made the request, it would have been hopeless, at least with that company. What's the message in all of this? Don't be afraid to tell the world what your needs are. As long as they are rooted in your beliefs and values—as long as there is no intent on your part to do damage to the company or anyone else—make your case. If you don't, who will?

I recently coached a client through a very similar situation. She had strong family values, but her work schedule was demanding more and more of her time. She was beginning to feel overwhelmed by all of her responsibilities. She wanted to reduce her hours from forty to thirty-two per week. What this really meant was that she wanted to reduce her seventy-hour workweek to something along the lines of forty-five hours. After conducting research on other companies where employees had reduced the number of hours, yet increased their productivity, we put together her case.

She went forward under the auspices that this was a "test." She knew that she was valued at the company, but she didn't know what the acceptance level for this kind of arrangement would be. I reminded her that she would never know if she didn't step up to the plate and ask. When she asked, she received. She successfully reinvented the rules.

## WORK, BOUNDARIES, AND CHOICES

Do you want more control over your life? Most of us would probably answer yes. The truth is, much like Dorothy in *The Wizard of Oz,* we've all got the power. We have always had the power. What power am I talking about? The power of choice. The power to say yes or no. It is so easy to get lost chasing the carrot. We lose sight of who's really in control. Finding your voice is very much about recognizing that you have the power of choice. Yes, you must be prepared to live with the choices that you make. But here's the good news—each and every morning is the first day of the rest of your life. If you don't like the way things are, CHANGE them!

[ Finding your voice is very much about recognizing that you have the power of choice. ]

The way our lives are today has its roots in our childhood. Women are particularly skewed toward the People-Pleasing Syndrome. The following story illustrates this influence in my own life.

"It started as a child," I stated.

"What started as a child?" questioned the interviewer.

"My need to please everyone," I responded.

"Why do you think you need to please everyone?" the interviewer asked.

"Because I want to be accepted, admired, respected, and loved."

"And you think that because you say yes to everyone else's requests, you will be accepted and admired?"

"Why, yes," I replied.

"Then why do you feel so out of control?" asked the interviewer.

"I'm out of control because I am pulled a million different ways and I so want to take care of everyone else that I am no longer taking care of myself," I said. "Quite honestly, I feel like I'm dying inside."

"Is that what you want?" asked the interviewer. "Do you really want to give so much of yourself that you have nothing left? Do you really think that people admire that kind of behavior?"

"I don't know," I responded. "I guess I hadn't really thought about it that way."

"Well, let me ask you one final question. Do you know anything about the Superwoman story?"

"Yeah, I guess I do," I said. "I mean, I know that people talk about women who try to do it all, be it all, live it all, but on the inside they want a life totally different, if that's what you're talking about."

"That's not exactly it," the interviewer said. "Let me explain. Superwoman was a really good person whose desire to please others was admirable, but she stretched herself too thin. After many years of pleasing others and taking on more than she could truly handle, she had a nervous breakdown, was committed to the insanity ward, and died. It was as if Superwoman had never existed. Do you know what people said about her death? The same people who called her and made a thousand requests that she honored said this: 'I thought she was smarter than that, to have taken on more than she could handle. It's no wonder she died; she tried to do everything for everybody. She should have had more respect for herself.'"

Is this what people will say about you? Will people talk about you after you have departed with a legacy that isn't worth replicating? If other people's reactions don't reach your heart, try and think of it another way. Would you want your son or daughter to repeat your behavior? My daughter has had such an influence on my life, particularly in the area of the choices that I made around my career. She used to tell me that she didn't want to be like me when she grew up. Every time I heard those words, the pain went deeper and deeper. Sometimes I even felt anger. Here I was trying to make life so good for her. I mean, I was working my fingers to the bone. I was sacrificing my life—all in the name of advancing her life. It wasn't until I got the nerve to ask her why she felt that way that I learned yet another lesson about beliefs and values. I really didn't want to hear what she told me. Can you imagine? Perhaps some of you have had this same experience. This is what she shared: "Mommy, you don't do anything but work. You don't have friends. You are always on edge." WOW! I knew that, but I didn't know that she knew it. That very day I began to make adjustments in the amount of time and effort that I gave to each facet of my life, including spending more time with her.

Do you have respect for yourself? Are you trying to play Superwoman? I was. Fortunately, my story didn't end the same way Superwoman's did. But, like Superwoman, I hadn't taken the time to really understand my beliefs and values. I knew what they were, but I wasn't prepared to apply them. I was using the wrong model. It took me eighteen years to figure out that I had no boundaries. I knew it, but I wouldn't deal with it.

Many of the women who were climbing the corporate ladder during the '80s and early '90s were experiencing the same thing. It was our first window of opportunity, and we were hell-bent to do whatever it took. There was a certain amount of conformity. We tried to act like we were men with wives at home to take care of everything. Unfortunately, that wasn't the way it was. It wasn't until someone asked me how my actions were impacting my children that I began to really look closely at what percentage of my life was spent at work. If my analysis was right, probably 70 percent of my time was spent at work. It's hard to have a complete life when there is nothing in your life but work.

Susie wears a badge that is self-imposed. Her badge is connected to the eighty hours a week she works, the sleepless nights she's had over the past two weeks stressing over an upcoming presentation to the president of the company, and the twenty pounds she's gained in the last three months. Not a pretty sight, is it? But can you relate?

How many times have you found yourself in the same situation? Why does it make you feel good to talk about how tired you are, how stressed you are, and how desperate for time with your family you are? It's a cry for help—an internal cry, that is. Many times men and women who are in the process of building careers believe that if they work themselves near to death, somehow they will get extra credit. *Newsflash:* You don't get extra credit! You aren't even thought of as "something special." In fact, truth be told, the perception that is formulated about people who portray themselves in this extreme, out-of-balance position is that they can't handle all the responsibility.

It's ironic, isn't it? Susie was convinced that she was adding extra value because she was stretching herself. Yet the exact opposite perception was being created. Challenge yourself to do a quick examination of how you would be graded in the balance department. If you are not happy with your discovery, make the commitment to do something about it.

[ Successful careers require balance. ]

Successful careers require balance. Is there an easy answer? NO! It's about making smart choices based on your life's vision. Balance is something I would love to say will come magically. It won't. In fact, it's hard work! It requires careful planning. It also requires that you identify some very healthy parameters. Some refer to these parameters as boundaries.

In a recent coaching session, I offered these suggestions to one of my clients who was struggling to find balance:

1. Remember what's important. Jobs can disappear in the blink of the next merger or acquisition, but families are with you until death. You want to have fulfillment in all areas of your life. Fulfillment and success require *prioritization.*
2. Step back and ask yourself why you have to work such long hours. Is it because there is a crunch project that has a looming deadline? Is it because you are learning and are going through a period of getting up to speed? Or is it because you enjoy the rush of being able to wear the badge that you *think* says to the world, "I'm slaving and you should promote me for it"?
3. Delegate when you can. The purpose of a team is to ensure that one person doesn't have to carry it all. Share the responsibilities and ask for help.

4. Establish healthy parameters or boundaries. As an example, if you have to work extra during the week, then weekends should be off-limits. Or maybe you could go in early two days a week instead of staying until nine or ten at night.

You'll know when you have found balance because you will experience a consistent burst of energy instead of a dragging tiredness and a feeling that you can never get caught up.

## Your Work and Your Life

Is the business world getting better about work/life balance? Absolutely. The fact that *Fortune, Fast Company,* and *Working Mother* magazines all survey the top companies to work for is fantastic. There is no need to work for a company that isn't family-friendly unless you are going to dedicate yourself to changing the environment and culture of the organization or your circumstances restrict you from relocating. This is all assuming you have the credibility and experience to get the kind of job you desire. Remember, the definition of a successful career is not limited to a title, a compensation, or a corner office. Successful careers are defined for each individual on a personal basis. It is the reason why a career strategy or vision must be a part of a life vision.

> Plan your life and let work take its proper place.

As you plan your career, decide how work fits into the rest of your life. Plan your life and let work take its proper place. Don't plan your work and expect your life to fit into it. I promise you, it won't!

To climb the ladder requires good choices and, sometimes, sacrifices. Before you leap onto the ladder, make sure you take the time to engage in the exercises included in this book. Don't shortchange this step—it's more important than you think. Carolyn's example drives this point home. Carolyn is a mid-level manager in a major consumer goods organization. She is married with no children, but she wants to have children sometime in the near future. She began her career in the field as a sales representative. While in that role, she caught the eye of a regional director who was in her territory and was really impressed with the work that she was doing.

Shortly after the regional director's visit, she received several other visits from key personnel from the home office. Not too long thereafter, Carolyn was promoted to a position in the city where the home office was located. Carolyn's husband was in the process of obtaining his MBA at the time she was promoted. He did not want to interrupt his education to move with her.

Carolyn and her husband made a decision together. They decided their marriage was strong enough to sustain living apart for a year. They understood that in order for Carolyn to experience the kind of career advancement she desired, it would be necessary for her to move to her company's home office. They both agreed that the sacrifice was worth the reward.

Fortunately for Carolyn, everything worked out as they had planned. She stayed in the home office, where she developed her skills, and was then promoted to the regional director position within two years. Her husband obtained his degree and then he moved to be with her. Carolyn's career advancement may not have come so quickly had she and her husband not been prepared to make some choices and sacrifices.

But not every story of sacrifice has a happy ending. Sometimes, even after you have made what you think are good choices, you find that the price is higher than you thought. Terri's story is like that. She, like Carolyn, was a smart, energetic professional. She and her husband, Dave, had been married for several years and had moved three times for career advancement, twice for Dave and once for Terri.

Terri had received regular promotions and was viewed by the organization as having the potential to attain a position as vice president. The one thing she would need to do was spend time in several different functions in the company's home office. The problem was that her husband absolutely loved where they lived and really didn't want to move.

After a lot of debate and serious conversations, this couple made the decision that it was in the best interest of the family to make the move. And so they did. But Dave got to the new city and fell into a deep depression. He became a different person. His negativity started to affect the children. And, needless to say, it affected Terri. He resented the move and the fact that Terri's career was now on an extreme fast track, while his career had hit a brick wall.

Terri made every attempt to help her husband assimilate into the new environment. She tried to help him find a job. She suppressed telling him about many of her achievements, and she never reminded him that it was her paycheck that was providing for the family. Unfortunately, no matter what she tried, Dave remained stuck in his depression. His unhappiness caused marital and family stress. After dealing with the situation for more than two years, Terri was faced with the reality that Dave was never going to be happy in this city.

She had to either find a new job or convince her company to relocate her to another city.

Terri's situation is just as real as Carolyn's. Both couples made choices, and both couples made sacrifices. One story turned out great, the other not so great. Why? Change is difficult for people, even when it is positive. But when one partner makes a decision to pursue career advancement, he or she must understand how it will affect the entire family unit. And a partner can't agree to a move simply because he or she wants to support the spouse; the move must fit into the family's life plan. In other words, a career vision has to be a part of a much bigger life vision.

This is an issue that many couples will face, given that married couples with children comprise the bulk of the nation's employee base. The exercises included in this book will help you design a career vision that is part of your life vision, and the exercises should be shared with your spouse or significant other. If you are single, you probably are not going to develop your career plan and life vision for the day when Mr. or Miss Right comes along, but it should be conducted with other particular elements in mind. These elements may include proximity to family, friends, city life, etc.

Recently I was speaking to a group of executives on career success and leadership. I made the point about boundaries and choices and how important it was to establish boundaries while building your career. I shared my personal story of how my son, who was born with Down syndrome, had to have surgery at the tender age of fourteen months. I had just started my career and was too afraid to ask for time off. I had been in the position for less than six months. I knew that I had been doing a good job, but I didn't think my boss would understand. I gave away my power because I didn't make the choice for myself. I let what I thought was the "pressure of my job" keep me from being with my son during his surgery. My husband went with my son, and I came to the hospital after my workday was over. Why do I share this story? Certainly not to be a role model or to boast about my wonderful accomplishments. I tell this story to men and women because I want them to understand that in order to have life success (personal and professional), you have to get up to the top and then reinvent the rules.

After the speech, a woman came up to me and said that she has heard many women executives talk with regret about stories similar to mine. She had children herself and she wanted to experience a successful career. But she felt as though she was in a catch-22. My first response to her was one of understanding. It was clear to me that she was in turmoil and pain. I asked her if she had taken the time to get in touch with her beliefs and values, and if she had set any boundaries. Even though she had tried to set boundaries, she feared not getting the next promotion because of her choices. Here are the points I shared with her about facing the personal responsibility of living your life the way you want to:

1. Identify your beliefs and values.
2. Establish your boundaries.
3. Decide where your career fits into your overall life vision.
4. Find other women and men in your organization who are faced with similar work/life balance issues.
5. Bring your concerns to senior management.
6. Look for small victories (such as being able to work from home a certain number of days a week).
7. Make sure your work is impeccable!

8. Make sure you clearly understand the measurements for getting promoted.
9. Find case studies of other companies that have done a good job managing work/life balance. Use these case studies to support your point.
10. When you get promoted, create an environment where the fear of not advancing because of family commitments is eliminated.

## Your Personal Boundary Protection

The next time you are pressed to do something that does not align with your boundaries, use this five-step process to help regain focus. I'm sure you've heard about "talking to the hand." Most people associate this with a negative, but I would submit that it can be a positive if you use it as a caution reminder. Think of the hand as your compass and make sure that the choices you make align with the keys for each finger. The thumb represents your Purpose. The index finger represents your Passion. The middle finger guides your level of Fulfillment. The ring finger can represent the Happiness that the choice brings you. And, finally, the pinky asks whether it aligns with your conviction to Service.

## Talk to the Hand

#1 The Thumb—Purpose

How does this current activity align with my life's purpose?

#2 The Index Finger—Passion(s)

How does this current activity or request align with my passion(s)?

#3 The Middle Finger—Fulfillment
Does this activity add energy for the fulfillment of my current goals? Does it align with my values, principles, and beliefs?

#4 The Ring Finger—Contentment
Does this activity give me a sense of peace and joy? (I know that I'm doing the right thing even if it means readjusting other priorities.)

#5 The Pinky—Service
Does this activity help me to make a positive difference for myself and for others?

Think about how many times you have checked the Caller ID, only to pick up the phone knowing that you don't want to talk to the Spirit Mom who's planning the next fundraiser. But guilt draws you in and you answer the phone anticipating that you will be asked to do something that will add yet another responsibility to your already overflowing plate. Stop the guilt trip! Just say NO! Or, if it aligns with all five elements, just say YES. But *say what you mean and mean what you say!* Don't just do it "because"! These five elements become a part of your boundary road map. Applying them consistently will give you strength to make the decisions that are necessary (including saying no) to get the most out of your life.

[ . . . say what you mean and mean what you say! ]

Now I don't want you to get the impression that you can go around all day throwing your hand in everybody's faces. I would strongly suggest that this be a *mental* process. One of my sisters (God love her soul) has been searching for how to establish boundaries for about twenty years. She is so deep into feeling as if she has to care for everyone else that she looks horrible, sounds horrible, and must feel horrible. Her favorite line is "I'm tired of being tired." And my favorite line back to her is "Then why don't you do something about it?" That is the question for all of us. At some point, we all have to do something that results in a positive change. If you don't get anything else out of this book, get this: *You are in charge of your life*. You are responsible. Yes, YOU! As scary as that is, it is also exciting. You are the architect—get busy designing your life to be the way you want it to be. None of us wants to get old and say "I wish I would have . . . "

## Keeping Stress in Check

Stress is a big component of today's fast-paced world. Success cannot be achieved without an adequate amount of respect for stress. You have to have a plan to keep stress in its place or it will take you over.

The corporate world is full of stress. There are outside stress factors and inside stress factors. You control the inside stress factors. You cannot and will not ever be able to control external stress factors. You must learn how to respond and process external factors in a positive way. One of the pitfalls of success is that you feel as if once you get up to speed, you don't want to get off the treadmill for fear that it will take too long to recapture that pace. (I can tell you from personal experience, this simply isn't true.) Everyone needs quiet, rest, and reflective time. It is yet another critical step in your action plan. We can't forget that we are humans. As such, we must take care of mind, body, and spirit.

Another reason to apply an appropriate amount of energy in this area is that we are examples for our sons and daughters. They repeat many of the habits and behaviors they learned through us. While we'd like to believe that's not true, just remember the last time you said, "I can't believe I'm acting this way. This is just the way my mother used to act." It's most natural to absorb through example. We learn by repetition. This is why it is so important to spend quality time thinking about what you want out of life and making sure that what you're doing is really what you want to be doing.

### Attitude Is the Key

Remember, you are in charge of your life and the way you want to live it. Know that what you want is worth standing up for. Following are six keys to keep your attitude right.

1. Listen to your body and mind. If you feel tired, pull back. Don't play the martyr. No one can help you with this except YOU.
2. Include exercise three times per week.
3. Set clear boundaries. Learn to say no.
4. Make time for family and friends.
5. Get fed spiritually.
6. Keep everything in perspective.

Another practice you might find to be of value is the use of affirmations. Affirmations are positive statements that help to subconsciously influence our thinking process. It is what some people call "self-talk." Here are some tips on developing and using affirmations:

- Make your statement positive.
- Make it present tense.

- Use "I" as a part of the statement. For example, "I am happy, healthy, and successful."
- Repeat your affirmation as a part of your self-reflection time or anytime during the day when you might need a little pick-me-up!
- Put your affirmations on note cards and place them anywhere that will help you remember to repeat them.
- Practice letting go of the past. Focus on the present.

[ . . . success requires resiliency.
Mistakes are great teachers. ]

I believe in the power of affirmations and positive thinking. Affirmations are still an integral part of my life. Why? Because there is always something happening that can cause anxiety. As Charles Stanley says, "You are either going through something, coming out of something, or getting ready to go through something." Discovering your values, beliefs, and life desires serves to lay a solid foundation—but sustaining success requires *resiliency.* One way you can prepare yourself to deal with the inevitable bumps in the road is to commit to adopting an attitude that rejects defeat. That doesn't mean that you won't experience failure. The difference between those who can bounce back from setbacks versus those who cannot is attitude. Women tend to hold on to mistakes like a security blanket. Let mistakes go. Men are great about being able to quickly move on after a mistake has occurred. Don't let mistakes cause you to think that you are not worthy of greater levels of responsibility. Mistakes are great teachers. There are secrets that can only be gleaned from the pain.

Shortly after I was promoted to a position as vice president, one of the major distributors in my area of sales responsibility declared bankruptcy. There had been rumors that this might happen and we were watching and monitoring the situation. As VP, it was my responsibility to make the recommendation about the best way to handle this situation. I deferred my decision to the credit department because I wanted to separate myself from the fallout. I was doing this because I believed that even if the account closed, these same people that I was dealing with would show up in other accounts. I should have never deferred such an important decision to anyone else. The distributor closed sooner than expected and we lost nearly $700,000. Fortunately, we got most of that back during the reconciliation activities in court. My initial guilt was overwhelming. I complained about the situation on almost a daily basis. It wasn't until my husband reminded me that I needed to get on with "the business of doing business" that I realized I was holding back my performance and my team's performance by hanging on to this feeling. What I learned from that lesson is this: Once something negative happens, there is nothing you can do to undo history. But you can learn from it. You can process the learning and put best practices into place that will prevent the same mistake from happening again.

## Smart Women, Smart Choices

The first part of this chapter focused on identifying your values and beliefs because you need to gain inner understanding to make smart choices. I truly want you to experience personal and professional success. It will require choice, commitment, and courage. I know it won't be easy, but it will be worth it!

When I started my career, there were no role models. There wasn't the wealth of online resources to help explain how the politics of the corporate world play into career advancement. And there was real resistance from the "good ol' boys" to accept, let alone embrace, diversity. It was the School of Hard Knocks. And you better believe that there were many days when I just wanted to throw my hands up and walk away from the whole thing, particularly when I was feeling like I wasn't being valued or respected. But I learned to look for that comfort *within myself.* You will have to do the same. It all starts with making the choice to get into the game. You can't sit on the sidelines and coast if you want to have a major impact.

In a conversation with one of my first coaching clients, Paul, the subject of choices came up. Paul holds a position as a director, working for a major manufacturer. He has worked for several of the top consumer goods organizations in the country. He is capable of obtaining a senior management position either for the company that he works for now, or for one in the future. The choice that Paul has to make is to consistently engage.

He admitted to me that he holds back and wants to fly right under the radar screen. When I asked him why, he responded by saying that he felt safe there.

"What are you afraid of?" I asked.

"I hate to tell you this," he said, "but I know that if I get into the game, there is a price to pay, and I am not sure I want to pay that price." He went on, "As a minority, it's been hard enough to reach the level that I've achieved thus far. I feel like I've gotten this far because I haven't challenged the system, even though there are things that I would really like to see change in my company."

Paul's honesty was refreshing. And his comments are more common than you might think. Leadership is not for the faint of heart. It is tough business. It requires mental, emotional, and physical toughness, but first it requires a choice. I told Paul that it was not for me or for anyone else to try to make the choice for him. He would have to decide for himself—as will you. If you make the choice that you want to pursue the executive ranks, whether in an entrepreneurial adventure or for a corporation, there will be a price to pay. There is a price to pay for everything in life.

The following statements will help you come to terms with your career vision. Decide if you agree or disagree with each of these statements, but don't stop there. Pause after each one and give yourself permission to relive previous experiences and to dream about what you want from your professional career.

- I enjoy being in charge.
- I am not afraid to challenge the status quo.
- I want to be known for leading or supporting a cause.
- I have a sense of calling to make a difference for generations to come.
- I am uncomfortable just watching the game. I believe my calling in life is to get into the game and lead.
- I am constantly seeking a new challenge.
- I am hungry to do something great.
- I am not afraid to stand alone for something I believe in with my whole heart and soul.
- I like helping others.
- I like making big decisions.
- I love being in the spotlight.

My career vision was to become a senior leader of an organization and then, one day, to own my own company. That vision is now a reality. Was I lucky? Maybe a little. But my outcome was more about planning, making choices and sacrifices, and a lot of hard work.

I felt extremely lonely in my personal climb. There was no one like me. I was the first crack in the comfort zone of the people that I would call my peers. The second break came as a result of my desire to change the culture from a good ol' boys' network to a far more diverse world that included women and minorities. In today's marketplace there are so many options to network with other women. Reach out and use every source. Join an industry association or a women's group. Sometimes support groups even exist through churches. You don't have to go it alone. You should network every opportunity you can. Set a goal for yourself to meet one new person a quarter to build your Rolodex—it will come in handy.

As well as I thought I knew who I was, what I wanted, and where my boundaries had been drawn, I found myself growing weary of fighting and often just going with the flow. As a result, I began to compromise my beliefs and even some of my values. I would curse like the guys. I would talk about others behind their backs. Don't get caught in this trap. *In other words, remain true to yourself.*

The one thing I refused to do was to adopt a sense of arrogance. I wanted everyone to feel important. I believe that every role in an organization has value. Every role, including the cook in the cafeteria and the clerk in the mail-room, is important to the execution of the strategy.

Make the decision now to build a career that enables you to make a difference for yourself and others. Embrace your leadership role in creating the future. Plan wisely and enjoy the journey day in and day out.

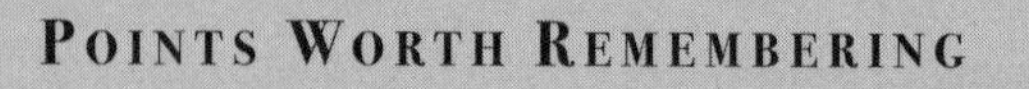

## Points Worth Remembering

- Building a successful career starts with taking personal responsibility for your destiny.
- Your values and beliefs are the nucleus of who you are, and they should never be compromised.
- You have to value yourself before others will value you.
- Don't be afraid to tell the world what your needs are.
- Boundaries help to keep your priorities in the "right" order and enable you to sustain success.
- A career vision must be part of a bigger life vision.
- You are the architect of your life and are empowered to design it however you want.

# Success from the Inside Out

*"The greater danger for most of us lies not in setting our aim too high and falling short; but in setting our aim too low, and achieving our mark."*
—Michelangelo

## A Portrait of You

With the material in the first chapter, we have established the need for a solid foundation. We can now turn our attention to designing the plan that will lead to breakthrough success for you. In this chapter, you will learn how to identify your passion and professional purpose, how to live your values in the work environment, and how to create a vision for your professional achievements. You are a mixture of your past experiences, your goals, your dreams, your fears, and your aspirations. You are where you are today because of the choices you made yesterday. Where you'll be tomorrow will also be decided by the choices you make today. To define how these elements play into who you ultimately become as a leader, you must first engage in a self-assessment.

Taking a personal inventory will be key in helping you to understand your strengths and your weaknesses. It is the first and most critical step in developing a personal action plan. It is in this stage where you will discover what you are passionate about and what really matters to you. Honesty is critical for this exercise. In order to chart your future successfully, you must be willing to take a hard and thorough look at yourself!

## Passion: The Energy Source

What is your purpose in life? What is the source of your passion? Review the list below, checking all statements that are significant to you. Add to the list if you need to. Then spend some time in reflection. As you go down the list, ask yourself if your current job aligns with these elements. If your current job does not allow you to achieve your purpose and live your passion, then it's time to take a closer look at what job or career will.

- Helping others
- Being a good parent
- Being a good spouse
- Achieving professional success
- Developing spiritually
- Maintaining good health
- Leaving a legacy
- Making a difference
- Changing the world
- Teaching others
- Inspiring others
- Learning continuously

Each of us has been put on this earth for a specific reason. By now, you know that I believe we are put here to make a positive difference for ourselves and others. But most people truly don't know what their purpose is. It's not because they don't want to know; they just don't take the time to think about how their lives can be used on a daily basis.

> [ Each of us has been put on this earth for a specific reason. ]

Think back to when you were a child. What things do you remember doing that made you feel really good? Was it taking on a leadership role? Was it singing in the choir? Didn't you feel just exactly right when you were involved in something that was important to you? Believe it or not, your career should give you those same feelings.

You lose your power when you are involved in activities that are not connected to your passion. I found this out shortly after my first big promotion. I had been appointed to the position of district sales manager in charge of eight people. All eight were men. None of them had ever worked for a woman before. They were quite vocal about their lack of desire to work for a woman. On my first day as manager, two of them told me that no witch was going to tell them what to do, and I shouldn't expect them to respond to my requests or my questions. One said that he would be willing to listen if I had the right thing to offer. Give me a break! You can just imagine what he was referring to. The remainder of the group just stared. Keep in mind that this was 1988—not that long ago.

After this welcome I was more determined than ever to show who was boss. I would make a request and include a threat if no action was taken. This negative relationship and negative behavior continued for the next three months. I struggled for the entire three months. Why? Because I had become disconnected from my passion. My passion wasn't about proving that I was the boss. My passion was to develop other people. It wasn't until I realized this that I was able to shift my thinking and my actions to reconnect with my internal power.

I recovered by demonstrating that I had only one agenda: to develop each and every one of them so that the team could produce more and all of us would reach our individual goals. I started holding morning "educational" sessions on consumer trends, organizational skills, cultural appreciation, and other relevant topics. The response was extremely positive. They saw that I cared. They felt my energy and commitment. As a result, the hard stance many of them took in regard to working for a woman softened. I continued to focus on the team's development. I purposely overlooked negative comments. I chose not to let the outside environment influence my focus. I was aware of the environment, but I was in control of the environment—not the other way around.

[ You're not ready to live your life until you know what you want on your tombstone. ]

This was a powerful lesson to learn. Fortunately, I learned it early in my career. It's hard to gain the knowledge from this lesson if you don't know what you are passionate about. So, what are you passionate about? And why? What makes you get up in the morning? What motivates you to keep fighting the fight to make the difference? If you don't know what your passion is, it is highly unlikely that you will reach your greatest potential. You may experience success at a lower level, but trust me, it's the pursuit of living out your passion that will give you the emotional energy needed to sustain your climb. Recently I read this very fitting quote by Charlie Jones: "You're not ready to live your life until you know what you want on your tombstone." If that doesn't drive it home, I don't know what will! Don't do what Oliver Wendell Holmes described when he said, "Most of us die with music still left in our heart."

Take the time right now to reflect on what you believe drives you. You might want to flip back to the first chapter and revisit your notes on your beliefs and values. Usually, your passion is rooted in something that is very important to you. And, most often, it's rooted in something that absolutely makes your eyes light up. You could talk about it for days and days until people tell you to SHUT UP! If you can't make this discovery on your own, you can seek help. Simply ask five to ten people you trust what words they would use to describe you. You'll be amazed at what is revealed. Somewhere in that revelation will be your personal power source—your passion! See if you can finish the statements below:

- I am happiest when . . .
- I feel like I am on top of the world when I . . .
- I'm passionate about . . .
- I believe in my heart of hearts that I was put on the earth to . . .
- My purpose in life is . . .
- My greatest strength is . . .
- I am absolutely no good at . . .

All of these phrases are designed to cause you to think. One of my clients said that when I asked her these questions it caused her a lot of anxiety. "Good," I told her, "then I know you are growing." Do you remember when you were still growing in height (not size)? Do you remember your mom or dad would tell you when you were complaining about backaches or other minor aches that they were growing pains? It's the same thing here. In order to grow, we have to be willing to experience a little discomfort.

Your purpose can grow or stagnate based on how you use your talents. You should feel good about what you do as a professional every day! The profession that you choose should serve to energize you, not drain you. If your passion is aligned with your talents, you will be able to make significant accomplishments in whatever field you choose.

### Finding the Passion to Fulfill Your Purpose

Let's build on the questions that were previously posed to you with yet another set of questions. You know coaches are known for asking lots of questions—so try to understand! This is a good exercise to help you get started living your passion and achieving the success you desire. Respond to the following statements:

If I didn't have to work for a living, I would:

________________________________________

________________________________________

________________________________________

________________________________________

________________________________________

I am able to perform at my best when the following conditions exist:

________________________________________

________________________________________

While I am alive, I want people to say this about me:

When I leave this earth, I want people to say this about me:

I feel most alive when I:

My greatest fear is:

[ I submit that in order to really know what you are passionate about, you must get in touch with your fears. ]

Did that last question surprise you? If it did, join the club. Most of us don't like to talk about what we fear. I submit that in order to really know what you are passionate about, you must get in touch with your fears. Your fears can and will block you from achieving your goals. Once you've admitted your fears, they can no longer control you. You can keep them in their proper place.

Getting in touch with your beliefs, values, and passions completes the first three steps of a five-step process. You should be proud of yourself for making it this far; most people spend their entire lives without truly knowing these parts of themselves. Now it's time to move on to the fourth step. In this step you will create a Professional Journey Map. Let's begin by examining where you are currently and where you think you want to go. If you are just coming out of college or an MBA program, the first phase of your journey might be to find an entry-level job. If you've been in the workplace for a number of years, you might be thinking more along the lines of taking on higher levels of responsibility. I suggest that you begin with the end in mind. As an example, I knew that I wanted to become a senior executive. So a part of my plan included identifying the skills and experiences I would need to get to the senior executive level. It's the age-old question: "What do you want to be when you grow up?" Start by asking yourself this: *What is my ultimate goal as a professional?* Use the space below to capture this answer. This is perhaps one of the most important questions that you will answer in this book. Take the time to answer it honestly and from your heart. Don't answer it based on what you think others want you to say; answer it based on what's inside of you. I recently asked my daughter this question. She is almost seventeen and I really hoped that she would want to graduate from college and then come into the business with me. In response to the question about her professional goal, she said that she wanted to teach psychology, coach a high school girls' volleyball team, and work with cheerleaders. She was pretty definite in her answer. It wasn't what I wanted to hear, but it was truly from her heart. Are you as certain about your goal?

________________________________________

________________________________________

________________________________________

________________________________________

________________________________________

Now that you've answered this question, take a stab at another one. *How does this professional goal or objective fit into my life plan?* Remember, you must lay out your plan in totality. Otherwise you'll wake up one day and be seventy-five and stuck in the "I wish I had" world. Believe me, there is a lot of regret in the "I wish I had" world. Make the decision today to pause long enough to ensure that your priorities are in order. If they are not, start doing something about it *NOW!*

________________________________________

________________________________________

________________________________________

________________________________________

________________________________________

*What skills will I need to accomplish this goal?* Be realistic! Recently I participated in one of my clients' performance reviews. My client, Kate, her manager, and I agreed that it would be of benefit for me to sit in. I gladly accepted the opportunity because I really wanted to challenge her manager to give her some tough feedback. After some discussion about business achievements, I asked her manager to describe in detail what he believed were remaining gaps that needed to be closed in order for Kate to advance her career and achieve her goals. What he told Kate was not what she wanted to hear. She thought she was ready for the next level. He told her that while her analytical skills were outstanding and her ability to serve as a catalyst was remarkable, he didn't think that she understood the basics of the business. Kate is an MBA graduate with nearly ten years of business experience. But her experience is not in the industry that she is currently building a career in. This was eye-opening for me because Kate had led me to believe that her previous experience afforded her the opportunity to cover all the basics of working in a manufacturer's world. Kate's goal was to become a senior consultant who would be involved in the design of the company's strategy. Without the experience of understanding how her recommendations would or could be implemented by the people who interface with the retailers, she wouldn't be viewed as credible, nor would her ideas be taken seriously. So don't rush to conclusions about what you think your skills are. Ask others, and if you can, use assessment tools to measure your abilities.

## Discovering Your True Talents

*What are my top strengths?* If you can't answer this question with ease, start by getting out your last performance appraisal to help you complete this step. Or refer to anything that you have submitted to your company regarding succession planning. Another resource that will help you is to conduct your own mini focus group. Pick three to ten people whom you value and ask them the following questions:

1. What do you think I am good at?
2. What two words would you use to describe me?
3. What do you think are my greatest strengths?
4. What do you believe are my gaps that I should close to improve my performance?

Now list the top ten skills that you currently possess (examples may include good communication skills, strategic planning, analysis, etc.).

1.__________
2.__________
3.__________
4.__________
5.__________
6.__________
7.__________
8.__________
9.__________
10.__________

Now, below, list your top five gaps. Why not the top ten gaps? I believe, as Marcus Buckingham states in his book entitled *First Break All the Rules,* that the focus should be placed on optimizing your strengths and neutralizing your weaknesses. I don't know anybody who has achieved breakthrough success by focusing on his or her weaknesses. On the other hand, I don't know anyone who has experienced success who wasn't aware of his or her weaknesses. The awareness of areas that represent opportunities for development can help you to a) make the choice to place emphasis on neutralizing the impact, and b) help you identify the kind of people that you need to surround yourself with—those who are really good at what you are really not so good at.

So, identify what you believe to be your weaknesses.

1.________________________________________
2.________________________________________
3.________________________________________
4.________________________________________
5.________________________________________

The best tools that I have used to help in completing comprehensive assessments are the DISCs assessment tools. Contact ASTD (Association Society for Training and Development) or check with the human resources department within your organization to find out more about DISCs tools. The great thing about these tools is that you get the understanding of how your skills translate into behavior. Understanding your behavior is what enables you to identify the best training/development programs to close your gaps. One of my friends designed her own assessment tool. She developed a list of questions that she believed would help her to better understand how people saw her competencies and performance. Yet another colleague created an assessment tool that he refers to as Start, Stop, and Continue. These three simple words can provide powerful insight. The way it works is that you identify ten people at multiple levels within the organization. Compose a cover letter that explains the purpose of the assessment and, most importantly, ask for candid answers. Have each person fill in behaviors or practices that you should Stop, Start, or Continue in order to be more successful.

To build a career that is based on your values, your passions, and your talents, you must be willing to take the time to engage in self-reflection. Let's talk about a process that enables you to gain a deeper appreciation for your talents. For me, the best way to get in touch with my skills has been to constantly conduct a self-analysis. In other words, I have continuously evaluated my performance as if I were reporting to myself. I have become my biggest fan and my toughest critic. I want to encourage you to do the same. If you adopt this idea of an ongoing self-analysis, you will never again fear performance appraisals. And you will always be able to market your achievements. We'll talk later about the importance of branding and marketing yourself. To conduct a self-analysis, all you have to do is—yep, you got it—ask yourself a lot of questions. Here are some examples of questions that I would ask myself.

- Did I exceed or just meet expectations?
- What were the business results of my performance?
- What skills did I have to use in order to achieve the objective?
- What lessons did I learn during this review period?
- What adjustments do I think I should make in order to improve my leadership capabilities?

Can you remember saying as a child that when you grew up you wanted to be a doctor or lawyer? Once you hit your teenage years, you suddenly realized that in order to become that doctor or lawyer, you would be in school for another ten years or more. And then you thought, "Definitely not!" But despite all of the challenges, there was something about doing that type of work that just stuck with you, something that really made you feel special, something that you wanted to do that made all the work seem like fun.

Recently a really good friend of mine gave me a very special gift. She gave me a smorgasbord of toys that were popular when I was a child. These items brought back so many memories and so many experiences that I had forgotten. I actually laughed and cried. This experience caused me to stop and remember what I said I wanted to be when I grew up. I remembered that I was an outspoken child. (That's probably putting it nicely.) At the suggestion of my Latin teacher, my mother put me into speech classes to channel all of my extra energy. I can remember giving my first speech and saying to myself, "This is it! I want to do this when I grow up." I discovered a passion to teach and talk at an early age! The belief that I learned about myself is this: *I believe that it is important for me to be heard.* That's why I talked so much. I had an opinion and I wanted to share it. What I found out as I climbed the corporate ladder was that people don't always care about your opinions. But once people truly know how much you care, then they will listen. I wanted to help people by telling them how to get better. Better at what, I didn't know. But my mother was convinced that I could make money talking. In a lot of ways she was right. In my current professional capacity, I do a lot of talking and a lot of helping. I am using my talents for the benefit of others and myself. How are your talents being used? Do you feel a continued sense of growth? If not, find out why not!

At this point of the book you should be getting to know yourself quite well. Some of you may be thinking, "But I already know this stuff." Perhaps you do. But I have found that it is really helpful to be reminded of these concepts from time to time, because the truth of the matter is sometimes we get so busy that we forget. By now, you should be able to clearly target the industry that you should be in, the work that you should be doing, and the life that you want to be living. If not, please don't go forward. Keep at it. Work through it. I just coached a brilliant young woman named Jane through these same steps. Jane is a finance manager for a large consumer goods organization. She is assigned to work on one of the largest retail accounts in the world. Jane is very good at being a finance manager. But secretly she confesses that what she really wants to do is teach. The problem is she doesn't want to give up the finance world. "Okay, so why can't you combine the two?" I asked. "Because I never thought of doing that and I'm sure the job doesn't exist," she answered simply. If the job you want doesn't exist, don't let that scare you. If you want it, go after it, build a solid business case for it, and, if necessary, create it.

## Focus on the Journey

The last step in our five-step process is to create your Personal Mission Statement. Getting in touch with your personal mission statement can provide clarity for the kind of environment where your passion, skills, and talents can be optimized. I can't tell you how many women I know who have resigned or derailed because they were in a culture where it was not possible to use their talents and be optimized. As you build your career, you will be tempted to take a job or a position because of a title. This is another trap to avoid. Mary didn't realize that she was falling into the trap when she accepted a role as vice president for a large distributor. The position was right up her alley. She would be in charge of a team of people. She would be responsible for building business. These were things that she absolutely loved.

She was so blinded by this great opportunity that she didn't slow down enough to check out the culture and the mind-set of the senior leadership of the organization. The story that I am sharing with you is a recent one. It took place in 2002. Why do I emphasize the date? To show you that as far as women think the business world has come, it still has a long way to go. Mary eagerly moved her family to a small city in order to take the job. She hit the ground running, offering all kinds of new ideas and best practices that she believed would accelerate the business. There was only one small hiccup—her boss didn't like aggressive women and he certainly didn't like the fact that she was changing all the things he had put into place. He began to sabotage her work. Fortunately, she had a Rolodex that was as thick as an encyclopedia. She was able to find a new job in short order. But if she had taken the time to make sure that the critical success factors she needed were in place beforehand, she could have saved herself a lot of time and pain.

> [Developing the career vision is great, but without the right environment you cannot be optimized.]

What has to be in place in order for you to be optimized? Do you need the ability to communicate openly? Do you need to work for a large company or a small company? Do you need to be creative? Do you need to feel valued? Do you need to work in an environment where celebrating differences is encouraged? Do you need a formal or an informal environment? Developing the career vision is great, but without the right environment you cannot be optimized. It's just that simple, yet that powerful!

A vision is what you see as the possibility for your career. The mission is how you are going to accomplish the vision. The mission is why you want to achieve your goals. It's the mission that provides the strategic direction. An example of a professional vision statement would be:
*"To be the preeminent expert in developing people by sharing knowledge, transferring skills, and identifying passions."*

You can see that's a very big picture. This vision will be in motion forever! You want it to be that big. You can't catch big fish standing on the shore. You've got to be willing to go into deep waters to catch big fish. Make your vision big!

Now let's look at an example of the mission that would go along with this personal vision statement:

*"My mission is to constantly acquire information, insight, and techniques to optimize the twenty-first-century workforce. This is the means to providing cutting-edge strategies and solutions to advance the performance of my clients."*

If you don't know where you are going or what you want, you will end up somewhere—but probably not in the right place. It's for this reason that I strongly suggest you engage in the development of a full-blown mission statement. Let this statement be your compass in the journey called your Career. Keep the following in mind when developing your professional mission statement:

1. What do I feel is my greatest asset?
2. What strengths have others noticed in me?
3. What qualities of character do I most admire in others?
4. Who is the one person who has made the greatest positive influence on me? Why?
5. What is the difference that I will make?
6. How will I measure my success?

### What's Your Story?

One of my clients came to me in the hope that I could help her discover her passion. She is a mid-level manager who wants to be promoted to the next level. When I asked her what mark she was leaving on her current job, she rambled. Then I asked her why she wanted to be promoted, and she rambled. "It doesn't sound like you know where you want to go or why," I told her. She thought that she was living out her passion by pursuing one promotion after the other. In her mind, she was building cross-functional experience and expertise. Cross-functional expertise is a great thing and you absolutely, positively must include multiple roles in your development plan. But in Lisa's case, she wasn't using the experience to make a mark or positive difference. It wasn't until the company went through reorganization and she didn't get the job she thought she should have that she realized people didn't know what she stood for. She got the news from her boss's boss. He didn't know where she wanted to go and he couldn't articulate what value she would be able to add. When you aren't clear about who you are, no one else will be either. I promise you that you will be a lot happier once you discover your passion. There's no need to wait until you are older and have experienced more; it can happen right now. Just take the time to find out. Your personal and professional life will improve overnight and be changed for the positive forever.

## [ You can't fight every battle. ]

There will be many battles in the business world. As a leader, you will be involved in making some tough decisions. In fact, many of the decisions that you make will affect not only your life but the lives of other people as well. You can't fight every battle. Don't even try to or it will cause immediate career derailment. Instead, ensure that you are using your passion and aligning your business decisions with your values and beliefs. When you put together your career plan, think about the mark that you want to leave. Think about how you can use your passion and talents to make a difference. Don't just go where the road is clear; take a risk and plow new ground, so that the mark you make will be permanent and will benefit others for years to come.

I've heard it said that you *know your passion is aligned professionally when you would work for free.* Since I value financial independence, I don't know if I necessarily agree with that statement. But let me offer a variation: *You know that your passion is aligned professionally when you pinch yourself and ask if you are really getting paid to have so much fun!*

## Getting to the Pot of Gold

As I have already shared, I am a big believer in starting with the end in sight. In the space below, answer these questions: When my career is over, what will I have accomplished? What will others say was my contribution? What do I want my contribution to be? What will mark my page in history? What were the steps that I took to get to the top and what did I do to make a difference once I got there?

______________________________________________

______________________________________________

______________________________________________

______________________________________________

______________________________________________

______________________________________________

## Points Worth Remembering

- Discovering your passion is the key to breakthrough success.
- You lose your power when you are involved in activities not connected to your passion.
- Pause to ensure that your priorities are in order.
- Optimize your talents by focusing on your strengths and neutralizing your weaknesses.
- The secret to a career compass is a well-thought-out and developed personal mission statement.
- If you aren't clear about who you are and what you want, no one else will be either.

# Personal Development 101

*"As you think, so you are. As you imagine, so you become."*
—Author Unknown

## Skills for Your Future

What will it take to get to the top? It will take competency, skill, and passion. Competencies and skills are developed through experience. Passion, on the other hand, is what is inside of you and drives your interest in developing the skills needed to climb the ladder. Passion can take you from a point of interest to a point of expertise. In this chapter I want to focus on your personal development process. Start by reviewing your list of professional strengths and weaknesses that you developed through the exercises in chapter 2. It is time to analyze how these will fit into your long-term plans for growth and success.

Employers need people who have a well-balanced mixture of experiences and skills. There are hundreds of different skills that should be taken into consideration as you assess your skill set. There are, however, some common skills that organizations seek in those employees whom they think are capable of getting to the top. The list includes:

- Leadership—the ability to persuade and influence others, motivating them to perform.
- Interpersonal Skills—the ability to build authentic relationships.
- Flexibility/Adaptability—the ability to proactively manage change.
- Collaborative Team Development—the ability to blend multiple disciplines and experience.
- Oral and Written Communication Skills—with a focus on listening skills.
- Strategic Planning—the ability to create a vision and a road map to get there.
- Creative Problem Solving—the ability to draw on innovative and creative skills to produce new outcomes.
- Culture Positioning—the ability to create an environment where people from all backgrounds, genders, and ethnicity can thrive and add value.

These are the skills that are essential to succeed in today's business environment. Savvy organizations recognize and value the education and training investments made in their people. Organizations are counting on you to put your skills into action. They are betting on the outcome that you will be able to use your skills to help others solve problems that will produce results.

[ Leaders have to commit to lifelong learning. ]

One of the challenges that you will face as a developing leader is the need for continuous learning. The speed of business will cause you to want to place training and development at the end of your priorities. WARNING: Do not do this! I am convinced that people who become victims of the "Peter Principle" (getting promoted to levels higher than their capabilities warrant) stop engaging in learning.

Leaders have to commit to lifelong learning. Set yourself an objective to participate in internal and external learning programs. There are so many options available today for advanced learning, including courses at prestigious universities like Harvard, Stanford, and Yale.

The very idea that continuous learning is not necessary is wrong. We live in a time of fast-paced change. In order to adapt to these changes, we have to learn and learn quickly. You should make it a best practice to read the newspapers that will help you advance. I read *The Wall Street Journal, Fast Company,* and, of course, *USA Today.* All of these publications are loaded with trends and information that will keep you informed. Make learning a best practice for life!

## Understanding Your Strengths

One of the first questions I ask a new client is "What is your number-one strength?" And most can't answer it. Some people will say that they are good at many things. Others respond by saying, "I don't know." If you are going to become a senior leader in any organization, you need to be able to tell the world what your strengths are.

Your ability to apply knowledge in a way that adds value to the organization is what they are paying you for. To prepare for a successful skills assessment, you may find it beneficial to review the detailed listing below for guidance.

## Value-Added Skills

| | |
|---|---|
| Organizational skills | Communication skills |
| Creativity | Problem-solving skills |
| Time management | Team player |
| Technical skills | Leadership |
| Administrative skills | Visionary |
| Change agent | Presentation skills |
| Role model | Public speaking |
| Good attitude | Dedication |
| Risk taker | Planning |
| Sets clear goals | Style-flexing capabilities |
| Asks for help | Listening skills |
| Decision maker | Critical thinker |
| Analytical skills | Financial acumen |

Take a piece of paper and make three columns. In the first column, list all the professional positions that you have held. In the second column, list the skills that you acquired from these various positions. Examples might include communications, project management, and strategic thinking skills. Another option is to list your previous and current jobs and list the top five strengths you needed to be successful in the jobs. Competencies are defined as the critical success factors that are needed to advance. In the last column, rank yourself as average, good, above average, or outstanding for each competency. This grid will give you a good idea of what your top strengths are and put you on the right track for completing a skills assessment.

| Job Description | Skills | Proficiency of Skill |
|---|---|---|

Once you have completed this exercise, you should be able to formulate a statement about your strengths. Some refer to this brief statement conveying your strengths as a "personal commercial." Others describe it as an "elevator speech." Regardless of what you call it, learn how to do it. In chapter 7, I will revisit the personal commercial and present you with an opportunity to build your own. Here is a good example of a commercial for a senior mid-level manager who is poised for consideration for senior leadership. Pay attention to the competencies and skills that are highlighted in this note that he writes to a potential employer.

*"I am an experienced, fifteen-year professional executive with expertise in sales and marketing based upon time spent with a global Fortune 200 consumer goods corporation. I offer superior skills in the areas of sales, marketing, strategic account management, people development, and breakthrough business performance. I have value-added experiences as a marketer, a wholesaler, and a manufacturer. I am an energetic, capable, factually decisive leader with a general manager's perspective, and I am a team player."*

WOW! That is quite a statement. This individual has solid experience and is able to translate that experience into a statement that has meaning. This is an excellent example of a personal commercial that communicates a lot of information about this individual. What skills do you think this individual brings to the table? Can you identify any areas of strength? Can you detect passion? Can you communicate what your competencies are in this manner?

The first step in communicating the contribution you can make to an organization is to figure out what your competencies are. Using the work that you completed in the previous exercises, pull out your top five strengths.

1. ______________________________
2. ______________________________
3. ______________________________
4. ______________________________
5. ______________________________

How do these competencies stack up against the competencies that your organization has identified as being important? Don't know where to get this information? You can start by examining the top leadership of the organization. Think about the positions they have held in their climb to the top. Another way is to ask your immediate manager. You might want to phrase the question in a way that conveys where you think you are currently and inquires about what he or she thinks is necessary to obtain the next level of leadership.

Detail one to three examples of how you have used your strengths to achieve your professional goals.

______________________________
______________________________
______________________________
______________________________
______________________________

What did you learn from these experiences?

______________________________
______________________________
______________________________
______________________________
______________________________

Detail one to three examples of experiences where you have not been able to meet your goals/objectives due to areas of weakness.

What did you learn from these experiences?

What can you do to capitalize on your strengths?

With whom do you counsel to ensure that you clearly understand the current perception of your strengths?

What can you do to address your areas of opportunity?

_______________________________________________

_______________________________________________

_______________________________________________

_______________________________________________

_______________________________________________

## What Problem Areas?

As you develop your career, there will be situations where you are not quite as confident about your abilities. The truth of the matter is that there will always be some areas where we are less effective than we are in others. Each one of us will always have some area of weakness. But on the other hand, failure is not all bad. If you haven't experienced some failure in your life, one of two things is true: Your goals aren't high enough, or you're not taking any risks.

One thing that can cause your career to short circuit is a need to be perfect. As a recovering perfectionist, I can say with a high degree of confidence that functioning, or even surviving day to day, as a perfectionist doesn't work! As perfectionists, no one, not even ourselves, can ever measure up to our expectations. Nothing is ever good enough. We are often haunted by the thought of what we didn't say or what we wish we had said differently.

> People won't want to take the risk of making a mistake if they feel there is nothing they can do that will please you.

I can't tell you how many people suffer from a fear of failure. To me, that's what drives perfectionist behavior. You want so badly for others to hold you in high regard that you beat yourself up no matter how good a job you've done. It's fear of failing that causes people to believe that if they make a mistake, if they are anything less than perfect, the world will come to an end.

As a leader, it is your responsibility to create a culture that is rich in opportunity for skill enhancement and contribution. People won't want to take the risk of making a mistake if they feel there is nothing they can do that will please you.

What can a leader do to overcome the perfectionism disease? First, admit to yourself that you have perfectionist tendencies, and then make a commitment to change. Once you've mustered up the courage to admit that you live and breathe for recognition of your perfect life but that you no longer want to function day in and day out hiding in your own skin, then and only then can you change.

Below are several steps to help guide you through your transformation. Make the commitment to practice these steps, and I promise you'll begin to notice a very positive change. You'll be calmer. You'll be more at peace. And, yes, believe it or not, you'll reach a point where you actually are satisfied. And when you make a mistake, you'll embrace it as a learning experience and move forward without beating yourself up. Although these steps are geared toward overcoming perfectionism, they are easily adapted to improve other areas of weakness, such as the inability to delegate or the struggle to incorporate honest, open communication.

1. **Awareness is the key.** You don't know what you don't know. Spend time thinking about your feelings. If you are constantly feeling like you're not measuring up, that's a red flag. Stop and check your expec-

tations of yourself and of the people who report to you. Don't just drift along assuming you are right. Look at your own behavior realistically.

2. **Make the commitment to adopt a new behavior.** The will to change any behavior is a choice. Make the choice and the commitment to change the way you react. In fact, stop reacting and start responding. Challenge yourself to set more realistic goals, ones that are truly attainable by yourself and others.
3. **Keep everything in perspective.** No matter what the fire of the moment is, trust me, it's not that serious. If your family is not hurt, if the sky is not falling in, and if you have breath in your lungs, then no matter how big a problem it is, you can deal with it. Mistakes are wonderful teachers. Embrace them!
4. **Don't assume the worst.** Emotional intelligence is all about your ability to process your own feelings and the feelings of others. Don't imagine that your mistake is causing everyone to lose sleep. You're probably the only one losing sleep. If a mistake occurs that affects your boss, the team, or someone else, simply admit to the mistake. Then take corrective action to prevent the same mistake from happening again.
5. **Practice letting go.** Once you have done your best, let God do the rest. It sounds like a cliché, but it helped me to realize I'm not in control of everything. In fact, there are actually many things you and I cannot control. Once we realize we don't have to be in control, we can begin to practice letting go.
6. **Listen for clues from yourself and your team.** If you hear directly or indirectly that someone who reports to you is experiencing overload, it's a red flag. Perfectionists always set the bar higher than is achievable. We push and push and sometimes we push too far. Look for the clues. If you are feeling tired or your team is complaining about being tired, step back and call a time out. Regroup and reevaluate where you are and what needs to be accomplished.
7. **Give others permission to call you out.** If you get past all the red flags but can't bring yourself to stop, then give someone else

permission to let you know when you are out of control, when your expectations are set too high, or if your deadlines are too tight. In order for you and your team to perform at their best, there must be fluid communication.

8. IDENTIFY THE DESIRED NEW BEHAVIOR. Find a mentor who is really strong in managing stress and creating realistic objectives and who has been really successful in leading himself or herself and others. Start mirroring the way that he or she handles constant change, disappointments, and problems. Try to adapt the behavior to your own style.
9. PRACTICE. Behavior is not easily changed. Give yourself time to learn and grow. Don't think that because you've made the commitment and want to make the change that it's going to happen overnight.
10. CELEBRATE SMALL IMPROVEMENTS IN YOUR BEHAVIOR. As you begin to take on and integrate new thinking and new behaviors, take time to celebrate the victory of positive change in your life.

In the early '90s I attended an executive leadership development program put on by the Center for Creative Leadership. I met a woman who is a friend to this day. She was an up-and-coming sales executive with a Fortune 500 company. She is a person who plays her strengths to the ultimate degree. She is really good at negotiations. In fact, some would describe her as an expert in negotiations. She knows that she is not good at putting a plan together to execute the agreement once the agreement has been reached. She shared her concerns about this area of weakness. We talked on the phone back and forth for months until finally one day she asked me to meet her in person and help her wrap her mind around moving from a outstanding negotiator to a person who could negotiate and execute the deal.

We met in a city that we were both traveling to. When we began to get into the discussion of what was connected to her underdevelopment in the planning area, she admitted that she didn't enjoy the slowness of the planning process. She shared with me how exhilarating the feelings of negotiating were. She also admitted that she was beating herself up for not trying harder to improve and that she was really serious about making a transformation. She talked about how good she was at so many other things, and she continued to express disappointment in herself for even having this area that needed to be addressed.

[ "Women may have to be better than some, mainly men, but they don't have to be and will never be perfect. We have got to stop thinking that we can be perfect. What we have got to do instead is play to our strengths. ]

"You sound like you think you should be perfect," I said.

"Not perfect," she responded, "but as close to it as possible."

"That's unrealistic," I replied.

"It may be unrealistic in your eyes," she said, "but women have to be perfect to get to the top."

"Let me stop you there," I said. "Women may have to be better than some, mainly men, but they don't have to be and will never be perfect. We have got to stop thinking that we can be perfect. What we have got to do instead is play to our strengths. We've got to use our strengths in a way that allows our areas of weakness to be neutralized."

Although she wasn't convinced, she decided that it was in her best interest to listen to what I had to say. "Why don't you think of the planning process as though you were in a series of negotiation conversations?" I advised.

"Because the planning sessions aren't like negotiation sessions. I told you, they are slow and boring."

"So, you are the leader. Why don't you change the way that the planning process works?" I questioned. She had never given herself permission to change the process. She had also never given herself permission not to be perfect. These two factors combined to lessen her ability to be effective in the planning process. Once she changed her paradigm about the planning work and approached it from a different perspective, then she was able to move forward. Did she ever become really good at the planning process? No, but she was able to modify her behavior to a point where she could be a value-added contributor. The point is you don't have to be the star of every show. When you are in a situation where work requires skills you know you are not that great at, simply adjust your behavior and draw on the things that you are good at. Apply the understanding and the methodology of the things that you are good at and you'll find a connection.

## Put It into Practice

Okay, so what are you going to do about the areas that could become strengths but just haven't been developed? Focus on improving one area at a time. Don't try to tackle everything at once. Keep in mind that you will need to secure resources to help guide your development. Find an accountability partner to help keep you focused and to give you feedback.

You will find that as you apply and develop your skills, you will be able to achieve better results. Getting better results, along with some other factors that you will develop from the exercises in this book, will get you the promotions that will lead you to the top. If you focus on adding one new skill set per year, you will build the capability to be a senior leader.

Keep in mind that, ultimately, to be a senior executive you have to able to address all facets of the business. You'll need to know a little bit about everything from purchasing raw materials to putting the end product or service into the consumers' hands. You want to be a generalist, yet develop an expertise that is tied to your strengths.

Take a moment to jot down your Action Plan for Improvement:

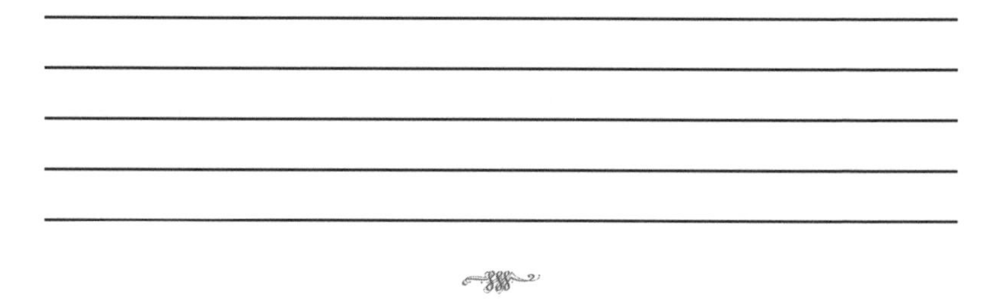

## Enhance Your Thinking: Create White Space

If you are willing to get down and dirty with yourself, then you will be able to reach the point where your confidence is rooted in the strength of your knowledge. Knowledge is something that no one can take away from you. Successful professionals are rooted in authentic confidence that is based on knowledge and substance. To build confidence and continue in your development, I suggest that you begin by reserving weekly time in your schedule that is just for you. This time can be used for several things, including assessing your skills, but you can take it a step further. Think about this time as a weekly personal growth and enrichment session. Think about a list of things that you could cover (not all at once) during this time. Here are some ideas for using this time wisely.

- **Scenario Planning:** Scenario planning allows you to mentally put yourself in different situations and experiences that have not come to fruition. As an example, say you've got an upcoming meeting and you want to make sure to communicate your point with power and extreme presence. Walk yourself through it. Analyze it thoroughly in your mind and make the necessary adjustments. When it comes time for the meeting, you will come across like a pro.
- **Analyze Trends:** If you are on the way up the ladder, you'll need to be prepared to have impromptu conversations about the latest developments affecting your industry as well as events happening around the globe. Make it a best practice to read articles, industry publications, and cutting-edge books on a regular basis.
- **Innovation/Creativity:** To really stretch your skill package, experiment with new ways that you can add value to your current position. If you can expand the scope of responsibilities and then convert that to a new process that would benefit the entire company, what a coup that would be! All it takes is operating from a position of "possibilities." Think about the problems you feel exist in the organization, listen to complaints from others, then come up with new solutions to solve the problems. Don't be afraid to be really bold in this area. Innovation and creativity are critical for success in the twenty-first century. The constant speed of change demands leaders who can think differently and challenge the old model.
- **Celebrate Victory:** As you apply this process and make strides, stop and celebrate—even if it's just for a few minutes. Women have a really difficult time slowing down enough to enjoy the ride. We translate celebrating into a big guilt trip. Lose the guilt trip. It doesn't add a thing that's nice, but it can cause you to adopt a mentality of never being

satisfied. If you can't celebrate the small victories, how will you be able to help your team celebrate the big ones? Celebrating success helps to build a reservoir of insight, lessons, and resiliency. Don't miss any opportunity to celebrate your team's or your own accomplishments.

## Points Worth Remembering

- Leaders must commit to lifelong learning. Make it a best practice.
- Being able to answer the question, "What are you good at?" opens the door to opportunity.
- Understanding and planning to your strengths is the key to advancement.
- If you haven't experienced much failure, either your goals aren't high enough or you're not taking any risks.
- Perfectionism is a deadly killer. Learn to set realistic goals for yourself and others.
- Allocate time for yourself to make plans and celebrate victories.

# Taking Control of Your Destiny

*"Don't sit down and wait for the opportunities to come: you have to get up and make them."*
—Madame C. J. Walker

## Common Threads of Success

Part of my preparation for this book included hundreds of interviews. The people I interviewed were as diverse as possible. I conducted the interviews mainly because I wanted to validate my thoughts before sharing them with the world, but I also wanted to learn. I wanted to understand others' concerns about corporate America. I wanted to get others' views on leadership, and I wanted to gain insight on common threads that were shared by those who had made it to the top. Some of the commonalities I found, not to my surprise, were that the most successful people I interviewed:

- Believed in self-leadership and self-responsibility.
- Were driven. They self-imposed specific goals with specific time frames.
- Were focused on competency development.
- Valued relationships.
- Saw flexibility as a critical requirement for success.

These are all behaviors and practices that must be applied as you step into the driver's seat of your career and begin your journey down the road to success. I share this with you at the start of this chapter that will focus on goal setting because I want you to think about these success threads.

## SETTING GOALS

You've been given the opportunity to review your personal choices; now it's time to determine how high up the ladder you want to go. You've gained insight on your strengths and weaknesses, and you've got a plan to continue to refine your skills. It's time to set a professional goal. I recommend you break this process into short-term and long-term goals. You can use this acrostic to help you define your goals.

S = Specific
M = Measurable
A = Achievable
R = Result-Oriented
T = Timely

S.M.A.R.T. goals will definitely get you going in the right direction, but let me share what I used as a guide in setting my goals. I used (and still do use) something I call a "R.E.A.L." goal-setting process.

R = Realistic
E = Energizing
A = Achievable and Believable
L = Lasting Impact

I developed this model because I believe that goals come out of dreams. Goals that are realistic have a better chance of getting accomplished. Let me give you an example of why setting realistic goals is so critical.

As you embark upon developing your career plan, make sure that you take the time to understand that life comes in stages. It's okay to have different objectives and goals based upon where you are in life. Let me explain this concept a little more. "It's a lot harder than I thought it would be to decide how to address all parts of my life," says Celine. Celine is a recent MBA graduate from Brazil. She's been married now for three years. Her career is starting to take off, but her husband is putting pressure on her to start a family. She says she used to spend hours meditating and dancing, but she doesn't do that anymore because of the long hours that she has to put in at the office. I challenged her to accept personal responsibility for designing her life to be the way she wants it to be. But I explained to her that she must realize that most people don't win the lottery and get everything at once. Most people go through stages in life where they get a little bit of what they want on an ongoing basis.

The way you get what you want in total is to have a plan. And your plan has got to have a timeline. The timeline helps to keep you focused on achieving your goals. Research suggests that the number one reason that goals are not achieved is because there is no specific timeline associated. One of the professional objectives that I set was to become a vice president by the time I was thirty-five. For most people this objective is aggressive, to say the least. Perhaps it was aggressive, but it was where I saw myself. The objective was achieved by my thirty-fifth birthday. In fact, it happened when I was thirty-four. I was the youngest appointed vice president in the history of the company. Did it happen just because I set the timeline? No, but without the reinforcement provided by the timeline it might have taken a lot longer.

Dave is an entrepreneur, or at least he thinks he is. He has set a goal to become a millionaire within the next five years. Dave has a high school education and has no desire to pursue higher education. He has limited work experience. He has a limited amount of resources with which to start his business. He has few contacts. He obviously has a lot of strikes against him. Is his goal to become a millionaire unachievable? No. Is it realistic? Maybe, but only if Dave develops well-thought-out plans that are built around goals that align with his abilities. If you aren't careful in this first step, you will leave yourself open to failure. You also need to experience some small victories along the way to your ultimate goal. The small victories serve to reinforce your belief in the goal, and they give you energy to keep striving to reach the goal.

[ Goals that are realistic and give you energy are goals that manifest themselves into significant achievements. ]

### Does It Give You a Rush?

Goals that are realistic and give you energy are goals that manifest themselves into significant achievements. But it goes beyond that. Goals that are R.E.A.L. will lead you to achieve breakthrough results. They become such a part of you that the emotional connection takes over and urges you on to bigger and better achievements. Terry, a female senior executive I interviewed, shared a perfect example that proves this point. Several years ago, she and a few others set a goal to gain the company's commitment to build a day care center for its employees. Her employer is the largest employer in the city where she lives. At the time, no other companies in the city had shown any signs of being committed to on-site day care services.

She was determined that one of the contributions she would make to this company would be a day care that would enrich the lives of the company's employees and make the employees more productive. She shared with me how she went about researching other companies that had on-site day care facilities. She was so energized that she found herself phoning companies and actually conducting interviews. The goal was accomplished within a twelve-month time frame. She experienced victories along the way that served to keep her and her colleagues on track. She was so proud of this achievement that she spearheaded an effort to secure a lactation lounge inside the main corporate building for new mothers. These two goals have had a lasting, powerful impact upon the organization. Her commitment to make a positive difference for herself and others resulted in several significant achievements.

She was promoted several times during the last year. Was any part of her promotion tied to her vision and goal setting? Absolutely! Successful careers are built as a result of many factors, including competence and results. But the significance of a career occurs when you go beyond what is expected of you from a performance standpoint. It goes to the point where you experience an emotional buy-in. You care.

What do you care about in your organization? What do you believe should be done differently? What can be improved to help the organization retain and develop its top talent? Maybe it's the introduction of flexible work schedules. Maybe it's the formulation of diversity initiatives. Perhaps it's a mentoring program. Or maybe it's a new best practice. Don't just do what is expected. Set goals that stretch you and others.

## Your Professional Goals

Answer the following questions:

- What is my short-term professional goal?

______________________________________________
______________________________________________
______________________________________________
______________________________________________
______________________________________________

- What is my long-term professional goal?

______________________________________________
______________________________________________
______________________________________________
______________________________________________
______________________________________________

- What action steps do I need to take to achieve both my short- and long-term goals?

______________________________________________
______________________________________________
______________________________________________
______________________________________________
______________________________________________

- How much time do I need to allocate for each step I need to take to reach my goals?

- What other factors will influence my ability to achieve these goals?

- How do these goals align with my strengths?

- How do these goals support what I want to be known for contributing?

Develop one specific objective to be accomplished per week and note it on your calendar. Mark a measurement date for a reality check each month until your goal is accomplished. Track your progress in a journal. What a wonderful gift this journal will make for the next generation! Perhaps it will be passed on to your children or someone that you will mentor for years to come.

Here is a set of guidelines for setting achievable goals.

1. Identify your goal.
2. Match the goal against your values, your personal mission statement, and your professional mission statement.
3. Share your goal with others.
4. Determine what resources are needed to help you achieve this goal.
5. Prepare for obstacles.
6. Commit to doing one thing that you can do daily to achieve your goal.
7. What's your activity for the week?
8. Take a temperature check (How does this feel?).
9. Make adjustments as necessary.
10. Make sure that the goal you set is your own.
11. Review your progress.
12. Reward yourself for your achievement.

## Balancing Act

There came a point in my career when I realized I wanted more control of my own destiny. I had been more than willing to make the personal sacrifices to climb the ladder, but I hadn't done a very good job of keeping everything in balance. I had been promoted seven times in twelve years, but it had come at a price. I was traveling at least 70 percent of the time. I would wake up and not remember what city I was in. I needed to step back and really think about my life and how my professional aspirations fit into the picture.

In a conversation with a very close friend of mine, we were discussing the challenges and frustrations of climbing the corporate ladder. I made my usual comment, which was something like "If only I were a millionaire." After a few sighs, I moved on to another subject. But my friend didn't let go of what I said about being a millionaire.

"Suppose you were a millionaire," she said. "What would your day look like if you were a millionaire? Could you really see yourself doing nothing all day long?"

"I wouldn't do nothing," I said. "I would do things that would really make me happy."

"And how would that differ from what you are doing now?" she challenged.

I paused and said I honestly didn't know, but it was something worth thinking about. What would your day look like if it included everything that you value and believe in?

I must admit I had been so focused on my career that I just sort of let everything else take care of itself. But things don't just take care of themselves. Balancing kids, a husband, friends, and other family time requires work. That's a lesson I learned that I want to share with you. It's great to build a fabulously successful career, but be sure to save some energy for other parts of your life. Live life to the fullest, but be careful to fulfill each facet.

One of the mid-level female managers I interviewed while developing this book put it another way: "I want to have a life while I'm young enough to know that I want a life." I thought those words were so profound. She is in her early thirties. She is married and currently has no children. I had given her the same exercises contained in this book to help her get in touch with her career and life aspirations. What she discovered was that she truly enjoyed what she was doing. Her favorite part was training other people to be more productive. What she also discovered was that too much of how she defined herself was attached to her career. She hadn't realized that almost everything she did before, during, and after work was all about work. She talked about how she found comfort in spending so much time at work.

I had her develop her own personal Life Wheel. (In a session with one of my current clients, she suggested that the wheel be turned into an umbrella, so here it is. The umbrella provides a great visual of the many roles that women must fulfill.) I had her set objectives for each area of her life, including Personal Time, Family Time, Work Time, Spiritual Time, and Do Nothing Time. Once she realized that she needed to learn how to balance the use of her energy so that she could have time for everything else outside of the work slice of her life, she began to feel renewed and balanced.

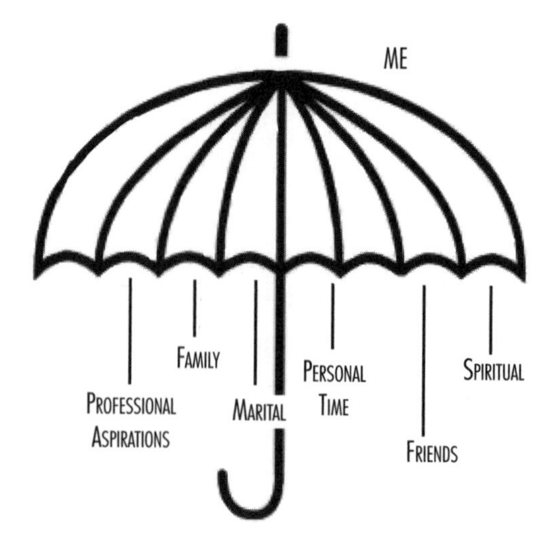

[ If you're working like a slave but then have nothing to balance it out, you could be heading for burnout. ]

The main purpose behind this exercise is to reflect on how the way you spend your time aligns with the priorities that you have identified as being important. The reality is that unless you set priorities for each and every one of these areas, something will suffer. Your level of personal and professional fulfillment is directly tied to managing priorities. And the truth of the matter is, the reason most of us work so darn hard is so that we can enjoy life with family and friends. If you're working like a slave but then have nothing to balance it out, you could be heading for burnout. Stop now and decide how you intend to handle all your areas of priority. You may feel this picture is just way too revealing. It is intended to be. Don't be afraid to admit that you are not where you want to be in terms of your life picture. Just take this as an opportunity to step back, reflect, regroup, and then reprioritize.

After she had completed the exercise it became clear to her that while she said that God, family, and friends were most important, she had absolutely no awareness of how little energy and effort she was giving to them. Whatever you focus on is where you will place your efforts. Success includes every facet of your life. Take the time to think about how the pieces of you will come together. Challenge yourself to set specific goals for each facet of your life!

The next step in our journey is a lot of fun and can be very rewarding. You have the opportunity to design your ideal day and your ideal week. You'll want to make sure that you pay attention to every detail. Think about the place, the city, and who you work for (someone else or yourself). What do you feel like, physically and mentally? Who do you work with? What kind of people are they? What kind of work are you doing? Here's an example of some of the components of my ideal day:

- I have time for exercise.
- I have meditation time.
- I have my own office.
- I have time to plan my day.
- It's beautiful outside.
- The room is cozy with warm lights.
- I work on seminars, speeches, and my book.
- I get to read before I go to bed.
- I have prayer time before bed.
- I get to bed by 9:30 p.m.
- I sleep in peace.
- I awake happy.
- I move gracefully, not rushing from meeting to meeting.
- I meet with diverse groups that are focused on getting results, not on egos.

It's your turn. Design your ideal day.

______________________________________________

______________________________________________

______________________________________________

______________________________________________

______________________________________________

______________________________________________

______________________________________________

______________________________________________

_______________________________________________

_______________________________________________

_______________________________________________

_______________________________________________

_______________________________________________

_______________________________________________

_______________________________________________

_______________________________________________

_______________________________________________

This exercise brings clarity about the kind of work that facilitates optimization of your strengths. It also helps you to understand the big picture. Take the time to think about each and every single detail as you describe this perfect day. Get the full benefit of this exercise by extending it to get a snapshot of your entire week.

Now that you have your goals set, it's time to pull the plan together. I only know of one way to be successful, and that's through hard work and a very clear plan. If you are willing to put in the time, you will see the rewards. I strongly recommend taking the time to develop a plan that includes the following information:

- Your life vision.
- Your professional vision.
- Your mission.
- Your goal.
- Ways to measure your progress.

Make the commitment to review this information on a quarterly basis. Be open to making adjustments as needed. Just going through the process of putting your thoughts onto paper can be a truly enlightening experience.

## A Personal Review Process

Now that you have clarity about what you want from your professional career, it is vitally important that you develop an ongoing review process. This is where your commitment to the process will be challenged. It's one thing to have clarity of the goal; it's yet another to do the things necessary to make the goal become a reality.

Here are nine keys to putting a process in place that will help you maintain your commitment:

1. Be your toughest critic and your biggest fan.
2. Build your own feedback process. (Choose co-workers, supervisors, or managers whom you know will give you tough feedback. Talk to them on a monthly basis.)
3. Look for opportunities to learn something new on a daily basis.
4. Once you've accomplished a goal, set a new one.
5. Build monthly self-reflection time into your schedule and don't compromise on this time.
6. Commit yourself to lifelong learning.
7. Challenge yourself to stay abreast of industry trends and developments.
8. Seek opportunities to identify new ways to improve the business. Don't wait for the new best practice to be formulated—you develop it.
9. Take responsibility for your own training and development. Identify the competencies that you are working on via the assessment process that was referenced in chapter 3, and then make a formal request to your manager to obtain authorization for participation in internal or external training programs. There are all kinds of development programs that are geared specifically toward women. Just remember that when making your request, you need to be careful to explain how the experience is going to add value to your performance and the organization.

## Points Worth Remembering

- A timeline helps keep you focused on reaching your goals.
- Goals that are realistic and give you energy are goals that manifest themselves into significant achievements.
- Success involves every facet of your life. Remember to give time and attention to areas other than work.
- Adopt a personal review process to help your goals become reality.

5

# Blind Spots and Pitfalls

*"Sometimes we can't see what we need to see even if we use a magnifying glass."*
—Gerdiest Reid

## Be Ready . . . You Will Be Tested!

There will be challenges and pitfalls as you develop into a true leader. Remember that you are the one who controls your ability to get where you want to be. You must "stay on purpose," as my friend Julie Washington says. You must be focused and deliberate. Your strategy must be crystal clear. And you must be unwavering. Even the best of the best have areas that need to be refined and developed. Often we can't see these flaws, but to others they stand out like a sore thumb. These areas are referred to as blind spots. Leaders recognize that overcoming blind spots requires outside perspective and coaching.

Blind spots, if not handled proactively and appropriately, can take you out of the game. They can undermine all the good that you have to offer. So can pitfalls. Some people call pitfalls "bumps in the road;" others say they are "valleys."

[ To sustain success you must be able to make a comeback. ]

Call them what you like, but for the sake of this book I see pitfalls as challenging experiences that you have in both your personal and professional lives. We have all found ourselves in a pitfall at some point in our journeys. What's important is what you do to get out of the pitfall. To sustain success, you must be able to make a comeback. This is what resiliency is all about: the ability to bounce back from challenging or negative experiences.

My son was born on November 17, 1982. My husband and I had been married for a little over two years. I was twenty-two years old. According to all the books and doctors, it was a perfect pregnancy. We were both so excited about the birth of our first child. The week before he was born, I was in the doctor's office for my weekly checkup. I noticed some information about mentally and physically handicapped children on the counter in the examination room. I remember making the comment that I was so grateful I didn't have to think about the possibility of having a handicapped child. The doctor had explained that most handicapped children were born to older women. I didn't give that discussion another thought until the day my son was born and the doctor came to tell me that he suspected Adam had Down syndrome.

Some doctors don't have any bedside manner, and this one certainly did not. He wasn't even my regular doctor. In fact, I had never even met this man before. He walked into my room the morning of November 18. I was breastfeeding

Adam. He came and stood at the foot of the bed. We exchanged pleasantries briefly. It was just a few seconds before he got to his point. He asked me if anyone had ever talked to me about having a child with Down syndrome. I couldn't imagine why we were having this conversation. He went on to say that he couldn't be absolutely sure until the entire test was complete, but it was his medical opinion that our son was mentally retarded. He called him a Mongoloid. He then said that most of these types of babies don't walk and don't talk, and that my husband and I should discuss the possibility of institutionalization. I went into absolute shock. Literally. My mind was not capable of receiving the information that I had just been given. I'm sure I was having some outward physical experience that matched the fear and anxiety flowing in my veins. The next memory I have is waking up to my husband and crying for hours.

> "The greatest measure of a man [is not] in times of success, but in times of challenge."

I'm not sharing this story with you to elicit any sympathy. My son is doing great. He is twenty now. He's done everything that the doctor said he would not do. Not only can he walk; he runs. He participates in every Special Olympics sport there is, except swimming. I share this story with you to help you understand how you can be going along with life, not realizing anything can happen to you. The news that my son was mentally retarded was a big challenge. It was a bigger challenge than I was prepared to deal with at the time. In one of his famous speeches, Martin Luther King Jr. talks about "the greatest measure of a man not being in times of success, but in times of challenge." The blind spot I had was thinking that something like this couldn't happen to me. Life is full of challenges—you and I are not exempt. But if your values and beliefs have been nurtured, you will be able to overcome.

It took me several months to begin pulling it together. Physically, I appeared buttoned up, but inside I was fragile. I tried to put on a good face, but it wasn't working. My sister Amberosine had come to stay with me. I had asked her to be Adam's godmother. With her in the house, I had to sneak to cry. Her presence was the source of my discovering yet another blind spot. I would go into the bathroom, lock the door, and have the biggest pity party you could imagine. My sister knew exactly what I was doing. For a baby sister, she's pretty smart. She must have been thinking for several days about a way to reach out to me. Her chance came the next time I went into the bathroom under the pretense of showering. She picked the lock and came into the bathroom, pulled the shower curtain back, and laid into me as I had never heard her do before. She challenged me to stop thinking about myself and start thinking about Adam's future. She told me I was wasting my energy and I was sending negative energy to my son. She challenged me to stop. I got the message, and from that day forward I transferred my energy to finding ways to improve my son's quality of life.

[ Who watches you with a truly objective eye that is not tainted by political currents or agendas? ]

I couldn't see that I was still in the fog. God used my sister to show me the way. This is why you need to have a really good friend or a coach who is willing to give it to you straight. In the corporate environment, most people will stand on the sidelines and watch you fall. Very few people will be willing to give you a true picture of your weaknesses. Who's your internal coach? Who watches you with a truly objective eye that is not tainted by political currents or agendas? If you can't answer this question, I would suggest that you take the appropriate action steps to find the right person to build this kind of relationship with. I promise you, the time will come when you need this person *big time*. Get yourself mentally and emotionally prepared so that you can respond with resiliency.

## Career Derailment

In one of my coaching sessions, I was asked what I thought could cause career derailment. I responded quickly with several items, but after reflecting on the question and not being rushed, I added several others to the list. Here's the first list. I'll call this List A. There is a List B to follow.

### General Causes of Derailment (List A)

- Unethical behavior
- Inflexibility
- Not living with integrity about your beliefs and values
- Not embracing self-responsibility
- Underdeveloped competencies
- Poor interpersonal skills
- Failure to self-market

- Selfishness instead of service
- Not aligning your passion and purpose
- Resisting diversity in its broadest definition
- Poor communication skills
- Fear of creating your own future
- Blaming others
- Blind spots
- An unwillingness to continually learn
- A lack of emotional discipline
- The inability to keep it all in perspective
- A lack of resiliency
- A lack of support
- A lack of commitment to the dream

Equally important to understanding the principles of building a successful career is understanding what can derail your career. I decided to develop a second list of reasons why careers can derail. This list deals with issues that are specific to the moment in time in which we find ourselves.

[ People want to be led by a person who is credible and trustworthy. ]

### Leading Causes of Career Derailment in the Twenty-first Century (List B)

- Endorsing a top-down management style
- Not respecting and valuing work/life balance and the inclusion of nontraditional necessities

- Lack of ability to build authentic relationships
- Believing that you can do everything by yourself
- Aligning yourself with only one sponsor
- Not developing cross-functional experience
- Holding on to information instead of sharing it because you think that it makes you powerful
- Openly disagreeing with managers
- An inability to adapt to change
- Not recognizing that people want to be valued
- A lack of emotional intelligence
- A sense of entitlement

People want to be led by a person who is credible and trustworthy. They want to believe with every fiber in their bodies that you, as a leader, have no hidden agendas. In today's fast-paced business environment, leaders have to increase their ability to lead others to action and to leverage individual strengths. You can't do this if you are harboring stereotypes and preconceived beliefs about women, minorities, or anyone who doesn't fit the traditional model. The emphasis in the twenty-first century is on knowledge and people. This means that you must develop great people skills.

> The December 2002 issue of the *Harvard Business Review* included an article about career advancement and the competencies that are needed to be successful. The article emphasized the importance of "interpersonal skills" as a critical component for any leader in today's environment. In fact, it was cited as a reason not to promote an individual even if he or she had every other competency needed for the promotion. A lack of interpersonal skills leads to arrogance. It also leads to self-promoting without the service element. Included in inter-

> personal skills is emotional maturity. The article cites the fact that most executives seek out smart, aggressive people, paying more attention to their accomplishments than to their emotional maturity. Emotional maturity is what enables you not to take things personally.

What's the impact of a leader who has underdeveloped interpersonal skills? He or she:

- Fosters an environment of distrust.
- Creates resentment.
- Reinforces power-based management.
- Serves to disconnect the leader from the team.
- Creates unhealthy competition.
- Encourages hidden agendas.

Being a creative analyst, forecaster, or innovator is great, but it takes relationships to advance any cause. In this same article, the author suggests that organizations that emphasize the importance of developing interpersonal skills and emotional maturity should include interpersonal goals as a part of the critical competencies. Taking the time to grow in this area is critical to developing your leadership capabilities.

One of my coaching participants, Susan, had a mind-blowing blind spot experience. The situation occurred in a review of a new position that had been added to support the company's overall strategy in new business development. Susan had been assigned responsibility for organizing the meeting where this new position would be reviewed and discussed prior to final approval. As directed, Susan set up the meeting for the purpose of discussing the full scope of the new position. In preparation for the meeting, Susan's boss, Ellen, had prepared an overview. Ellen had her own secretary distribute the overview, but Ellen didn't put her name on the document. Susan arrived early and began to read the document and commenced to use a red pen to mark her comments onto the document. Shortly thereafter, Ellen entered the room. She immediately noticed the huge red lines that Susan had placed all over the document. As soon as Ellen sat down, Susan began to share her insights and disappointments. Her boss patiently listened and then responded with a question. She asked Susan how what she had just shared with the group differed from what was on the document. Susan really couldn't articulate any key differences. After she stumbled all over herself, Ellen formally opened the meeting by sharing that she had been the one who drafted the document. Everyone could see every ounce of blood in Susan's body ooze down to her toes. Why did this happen? Susan got so focused on getting her point across that she blinded herself. She didn't even think. That's what happens when you hit a blind spot. You don't think about how what you are doing will have an impact on others.

What should Susan have done? She should have sought to understand the viewpoints of the person who created the document. She should have voiced her concerns in the forms of questions rather than statements. She should have taken the time to think about the impact of her words on others. Her choices did not position her as a leader. Instead, they positioned her as an insensitive, egotistical, self-serving individual.

How many times have you made comments that didn't position you well? You never know who is listening or who will be impacted by your words. Leaders always have to choose their words wisely. If your words come across void of sensitivity to others, you can expect that people will quickly begin to tune you out. As a result, you will be ineffective.

Make a personal commitment to yourself to spend some time thinking about how you come across. Ask for input from others. You might start with the following exercise. What you want to get out of this exercise is an honest assessment of the perceptions you create as a result of your words and actions. I suggest that you first answer these questions yourself and then ask someone else to answer these questions about you.

1. How often do you hear people say to you, "I can't believe you just said that"?
2. Do you communicate with an appreciation for the feelings of those who are receiving the message?
3. Do you blame others for project outcomes that don't meet expectations without first examining what contributions (positive and negative) you've made?
4. Do you acknowledge your leadership on projects while also giving credit to the key accomplishments made by each team member?
5. Do you resent it when others have the limelight?
6. Do you always believe that your answer is the only right answer?
7. Do you intentionally undermine other people's ideas because you need to always be the center of attention?
8. Do you find yourself experiencing physical or emotional distress in reaction to an idea that is shared by someone else?
9. When someone presents with a passionate delivery (especially a woman), do you find yourself saying, "She's got her hair on fire," instead of trying to understand where she is coming from?
10. When your counterparts are presenting, do you find yourself thinking, "Oh, they are just big suck-ups"?
11. Do you believe that what you put out will come back to you (good or bad)?
12. Do you set out each day to use your talents and gifts to make a difference for others?

13. Do people tell you that you are a caring person?
14. Are you always under pressure?
15. Do you listen with an open ear and a sincere wish to be influenced by the thoughts of others?
16. Are you sometimes not prepared and do you try to dance your way out of direct questions?
17. Do you openly put other people down?
18. Do you openly admit to mistakes?
19. Are you comfortable with saying, "I don't know," as a response?
20. Do you treat senior leaders in the organization better than you treat the mail clerk?

Answering these questions honestly will get you started on gaining an appreciation for those sides of your character that might not be serving you well. Then you've got to be willing to do something about it. You've got to be willing to learn to bend and mold yourself to become a better person, a stronger leader, and a candidate to rise to the top of any organization.

## Watch Out for the Quicksand

There are more snakes in corporate America than you can imagine. As long as there are people who want power, there will be politics. Somebody always wants to be top dog. It's important to be aware of the political structure within your organization. It's a not-so-apparent part of the culture in most organizations. Trying to play the politics game is a big pitfall waiting to suck you up. Don't do it. Don't spend your time or energy on things you cannot control. Politics is one of those things that you absolutely cannot control. Without insight as to who is the king (or possibly queen) politician of the day, you could insult or put down someone who is connected to someone else and find yourself in a heap of trouble. My advice: *Always take the high road.* Make friends at every level of the organization. Treat everyone the same.

[ Don't spend your time or energy on things you cannot control. ]

I have seen many situations where an individual thought he or she had been inducted as a key political player, but he or she couldn't have been more wrong. And the consequence? Career derailment. Several years ago, I witnessed this in a most powerful way. David was a mid-level manager who had been handpicked by one of the senior vice presidents (SVPs) to become his right-hand man. David was not the sharpest individual I had ever met, but he had a keen understanding of technology. This was his gift. The position he held didn't really optimize his technological skills. Instead, he was managing people and serving as the gofer for the SVP. He was a decent fellow, but he had no personality at all. So why would they put him in charge of people?

The SVP would often send David to participate in meetings that he could not attend. This gave David a false sense that he was in a protected class or group. On several occasions David's underdeveloped interpersonal skills got the best of him. He got into a heated exchange with another SVP about a new initiative that was going to involve sales and information technology. This was not the first time David had expressed himself as the technology expert. Unfortunately, he had taken a stand that was incorrect. He was right in expressing his concern about the technology portion of the initiative, but he lacked the experience from the end-user side. As a result, he was totally off-base in his position and his argument. It was not his natural personality to express himself in such a bold manner. But his false sense of protection gave him a surge of confidence.

The first time David's boss was approached with complaints about David, he did extend a blanket of protection. The second time it happened, he began to distance himself from David. It wasn't too long thereafter that other SVPs started spurting out sound bites that were negative about David. The negative press was getting hotter and hotter. David appealed to the SVP whom he thought was his protector. The response he got absolutely blew his mind. The SVP told him that he had crossed the line and that he was damaged goods. Not too long after that, David was demoted.

What happened? David tried to play the game and got burned. It's that simple. He let his arrogance get in the way of seeing the landscape for what it really was. Don't ever get so full of yourself that you think you are protected. Having said that, I will offer you insight on a few ways you can sharpen your awareness of the political game. This advice is not intended to help you play the game. I absolutely hate it. I hate it with every fiber in my body. If we as humans could ever realize that we are on the same team, I can't begin to imagine the kinds of profound accomplishments that would become reality. These insights are being provided to keep your career on track and shield you from career derailment.

- Develop relationships at every level of the organization.
- Always convey the point that you accept personal responsibility for your career.
- Stay focused on functions that add value.
- Manage conflict in a spirit of respect for the other person.
- Become a student of reading in between the lines.

- Don't count on anyone to protect you.
- Don't ever assume that just because you are intelligent, people will put up with arrogance or ego.
- Only fight the battles that you feel passionate about and when you know, based upon research, that your position adds value to the organization.

### Emotional Discipline

One of the fastest ways to derail a career is to focus on negative experiences, negative people, or negative environments. In order to effect change, you have to be in control of yourself. That means being able to handle conflict, put-downs and belittlement with emotional discipline. We have already established the importance of relationships in building successful careers. Relationships inside the corporate world, just like those outside, require work, patience, and forgiveness. It's just a lot harder to apply patience and forgiveness to someone you don't call family. But the truth of the matter is that the people you work with are a lot like family—just in a different way.

> If you find yourself experiencing a constant loss of energy or if you are agitated a lot, maybe you are guilty of taking things too personally and need to fine-tune your emotional intelligence skills.

My own experience is that men are much better at this than women. There is also quite a bit of research to support this thought. Men can scream at each other and put down each other's ideas and it's called bantering. Once the day is through, men are able to put the bantering behind and go out for a drink. Why? They don't take it personally. On the other hand, women are quite different in this area. We take insults or idea put-downs as a personal assault on who we are. It took me a long time to realize that I was harboring resentment about negative statements that had been made about me. I didn't want to admit that I would look at my counterparts and wonder, "How can I get you back for that sly statement you made at the meeting last week?" Don't get sucked up into this trap. You need all the energy you can muster to be effective.

If you find yourself experiencing a constant loss of energy or if you are agitated a lot, maybe you are guilty of taking things too personally and need to fine-tune your emotional intelligence skills. Challenge yourself to keep your emotions in check. Note your response to the following statements and try to maintain a high level of awareness in this area.

- I am able to remain calm and composed under pressure.
- I am able to process negative feelings without becoming distressed.
- I am able to maintain focus despite chaos around me.
- I am not afraid to admit to my mistakes and use them as a learning opportunity.
- I can take constructive feedback without becoming depressed or defensive.
- I am aware of how my behavior negatively or positively impacts someone else.
- I resist the temptation to jump to conclusions.
- I can process anger in a healthy way.

I cannot begin to tell you how much time is wasted in corporate America as a result of people trying to "one-up" their counterparts. It's an absolute crime. I don't care if you are male or female, it is important to put aside childish tendencies and stay focused on the business. Today's workforce needs collaboration to experience success. You can't collaborate if you are busy trying to outdo each other. I think it will take organizational compensation retooling in order for change to be drilled into the deepest levels in this area. Instead of rewarding people for individual performance, companies should reward team performance. This would drive the right behavior. We have got to find a way to clear up misunderstandings quickly, but to do so we have to create an environment where learning is encouraged. We have to create an environment where teams are willing to find ways to build on each other's ideas rather than tearing them down.

Let me give you an example of the damage to productivity that occurs as a result of people harboring resentment. Don is a vice president of sales working for a large manufacturing company. He has nine direct reports. The team has been working on developing a new process for introducing promotional products into the marketplace. The company has had numerous miscalculations during the promotional planning process. These miscalculations have resulted in huge financial loss to the company. They have damaged external relationships and strained internal relationships as well.

Don openly favors one of his direct reports, Paul. Don often meets alone with Paul, discussing strategies and plans that should be discussed with the group at large. This activity builds a tremendous amount of resentment between Paul and the rest of the team. The resentment builds to the point that Paul is nicknamed "Suck Up." Paul loves the attention from Don and the feeling of being "special" and does nothing to build relationships with his counterparts. Don often has Paul start the meetings until he is able to get there. This builds even more resentment among the team.

The tension comes to a head as the new promotional process is being finalized. The majority of the team, with the exception of Paul, believes that together they have developed a program that will improve the overall efficiency of promotional product activities throughout the country. But Paul disagrees. He points out that there are production concerns that would limit the effectiveness of the process. His counterparts believe that in order for the organization to meet the needs of the consumer, the production department will have to find a way to make the necessary adjustments to accommodate the program requirements. Don, in his usual but unfortunate style, defers to Paul. Don decides that the company should not move forward with the new plan until a comprehensive production review has been conducted.

The team is devastated. They know that not making these changes will result in product overstocks that will have an extremely negative impact upon the supply chain and the company's deteriorating reputation. They also realize that sales will be negatively affected, which will make it that much harder to reach the sales targets for the year. The team believes that the production department would be more than willing to find a way to make the necessary changes. They also believe that the only reason Paul didn't want to go forward with the plan was so that he could look as if he was a big-picture thinker. He also wanted to demonstrate that he was powerful, because Don defers to his judgment more than he does to the team's judgment. Don's decision to support Paul's position causes the rest of the team not to feel valued.

As a result, the team begins to pull back and does not offer new ideas. Inability to harness the full talents and input of the entire team negatively impacts innovation, creativity, and breakthrough results.

This is how powerful resentment can be. It can cause dissension, frustration, and unnecessary stress. Don had a blind spot that caused him to make decisions that were not in his best interest or the group's best interest. The group's ability to produce great results was compromised because they resented the favoritism. And they resented Paul for leveraging his relationship with the boss. In this example, the team lost focus on what was most important—doing the right thing to get the best results. The effective leaders of the twenty-first century will build collaborative teams where input from everyone is valued. Favoritism will be diminished as a result of each individual being included, respected, and valued for his or her unique input. If you want to see productivity increase, if you want to see breakthrough results, eliminate resentment and build collaborative teams.

## Points Worth Remembering

- Overcoming blind spots often requires outside perspective and coaching. You must be able to make a "comeback."
- Lack of interpersonal skills can result in arrogance and self-promotion.
- Interoffice politics are a big pitfall; don't play that game.
- Nurture relationships at every level of the organization, and treat everyone the same.
- Develop emotional discipline to avoid taking statements or situations personally.

# The Power of Positive Communication

*"How well we communicate is determined not by how well we say things, but by how well we are understood."*

—Andy S. Grove

## Express Yourself

What career development book would be complete without a chapter on communication? After all, it is how we get things done. The way we present ourselves and our success directly ties into our ability to be effective at both oral and written communications. Communication is part of what enables us to connect with others. It is what enables us to share, to learn, and to grow. Whether through words, body language, tone of voice, or other expressions of communication, we have the power to make a positive change for ourselves and for others. One of my colleagues is an excellent communicator. She says that the reason why people are underdeveloped in their communication skills is because they assume too much. People assume that what they say is heard the way it is intended to be heard. Miscommunication is the source of lost productivity. In fact, I believe that a lot of the problems that occur in corporate America are the direct result of either poor communication or a lack of communication.

> Miscommunication is the source of lost productivity.

According to Warren Bennis, "Leaders are people who are able to express themselves fully . . . they know who they are, what their strengths and weaknesses are, and how to fully deploy their strengths and compensate for their weaknesses. They also know what they want, why they want it, and how to communicate what they want to others in order to gain their cooperation and support. Finally, they know how to achieve their goals."

For women, communication has always been a sore area of discussion. We have a history of belittling our accomplishments by using weak words and by being too flowery or long-winded. Communication is at the center of everything we do. It is so important for women to be masters at communicating. In order to advance, you must be able to sell your ideas, concepts, and vision. One of the major responsibilities of a leader is to foster change. The best way to get this done and translated into real action is through positive communication.

Effective communication will enable you to share your passion and leadership vision within the organization. I am amazed at how many people don't know how to let the world know what they want. I have learned in my climb up the ladder that no one can speak for you like you can speak for yourself. Sometimes people are not open in their communications because they think that they have to keep their game faces on in the work environment. This often leads people to keep their guard up. Then it leads to distrust. It's hard to make connections in an environment where people don't feel as if they can truly be themselves or be open.

[ I am amazed at how many people don't know how to let the world know what they want. ]

About a year ago, I began coaching two female clients who worked for the same company. These two individuals had very similar backgrounds that included cross-functional expertise. Both of them were fairly well known and respected for their work throughout the organization. And, believe it or not, they were friends and were open with each other about the fact that they wanted the same job. I coached each of them on individual areas of performance enhancement. And I gave each of them the same counsel about the importance of communicating their career advancement objectives to the right people.

After several months passed, each saw her individual performance improve. Unfortunately, only one of them heeded my advice to get out and tell the world about how these new skills enhanced her ability to add more value to the organization and why these skills positioned her for the next level. The other coaching participant relied on her boss to spread the good news. Her strategy backfired. Ultimately, the coaching participant who got out and spoke on her own behalf was promoted. What's the lesson to be learned? Climbing the ladder requires exceptional communication.

Every word that comes out of your mouth sends signals to the world about who you are, what you believe, and what you value. The ability to speak with conviction gives you confidence and builds a very positive image of your capabilities. I encourage my clients to identify and adopt language that reflects who they are. As an example, I use connecting words or phrases like "based upon research," or "analysts suggest," so that what I'm about to say is connected with a source that the audience already gives credibility. I also use phrases like "to the best of my memory," so that if I don't remember something correctly I have an out. There are some communication best practices that women need to reach out and grab hold of. I have merely outlined the top areas that you should focus on. This is not by any means a comprehensive list. I challenge you to reflect on your current communication style and identify the areas that you are really good at, and those areas that need some polishing.

## Weak Words

How many times have you heard women in a meeting say, "I'm sure that you have already thought of this, but one of the ideas I had was to . . . " This kind of phraseology discounts her contribution and makes her look weak. Or how many times have you heard women respond to a question by beginning with the words, "I think . . . " instead of, "There is an argument for . . . " What about words like "Maybe," or "Really, you just aren't getting what I'm saying."

Women need to use bold language that conveys leadership and knowledge of the situation. Compare these two statements:

"I guess it would be a good idea to ensure that everyone is going after the same goal."

"It is vitally important for our performance that each and every team member be focused on achieving the same goal."

Can you see the difference? The first example projects an image of a person who is not quite sure why everyone should be on the same page, while the second example displays boldness and leadership. In the second example the communicator demonstrates a sense of urgency and a call to action.

Do you use weak words? What are some examples that you can remember where you used weak language? What changes do you need to make to your communication style to eliminate weak words?

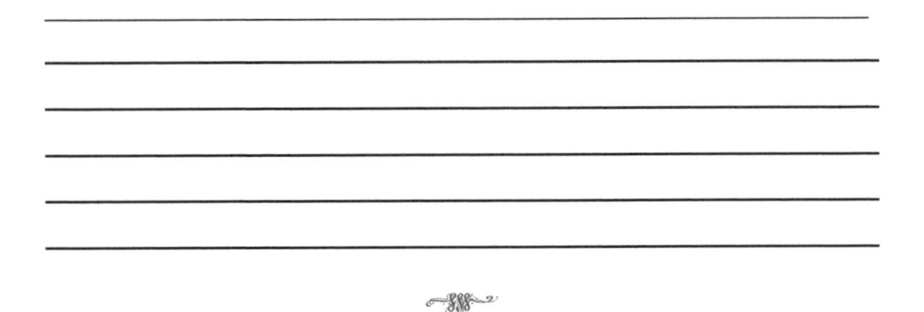

## What Body Language Do You Speak?

Are you someone who picks and pulls at herself? You might not think so, but think about how many times you touch your hair, push your sleeves back, or play with your jewelry. I have seen all three done by the same person while she was making a presentation. All of these kinds of activities are about nervous tension and a lack of awareness. I have even heard women break out in laughter while they are presenting or talking to someone. These are gestures that minimize your impact with the audience.

Given that you may not be aware of these habits, I am going to suggest that you find another female that you trust who attends functions or meetings with you to be your accountability partner in this area. Ask this person to observe you in action, looking closely for inappropriate gestures that damage your image. Record your findings, and if necessary, practice in front of a mirror until you are keenly aware of your physical behaviors.

## Miss Apologetic

As a leader, people will respond to your direction and guidance. I can't tell you how bad it sounds when you are the person in charge and you apologize to your team because you have to ask them to do things to advance the business. I have had many clients tell me that the reason they apologize is because they don't want to come across like a bossy witch. Okay, hear this: You have to be able to get people to take action, but that doesn't mean you have to be bossy or apologetic. Instead, you need to be respectful, yet direct.

These two examples illustrate the point:

> "Sally, would you, do you think that you might find time today to get these reports together? I have to give them to the senior vice president."
>
> "Sally, I'm sure that you have a lot on your plate already. Please put getting these reports together for the senior vice president at the top of the list. He needs these to make several key business decisions. Sally, I really appreciate all your hard work."

As you can see, in the first example the image is of a weak leader. The second example portrays a sensitive but firm leader who knows what needs to be done. When communicating a request, just remember to do the following:

1. Acknowledge work that is already in progress.

2. Explain what you need and why you need it.
3. Provide time sensitivities.
4. Openly value the person for the work that they do.

Is this an area of strength or weakness for you? Use the space below to capture your thoughts and plans for behavior adjustments in this area.

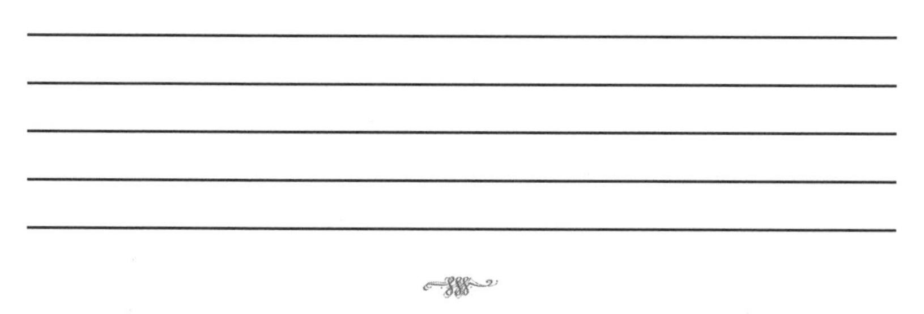

## Miss Cheerleader

Special note: This is not a put-down for young women who are cheerleaders. My daughter is captain of her varsity cheerleading squad and a bona fide athlete. I am extremely proud of her. I learned a lot from my own experience as a Tulane cheerleader. What I'm referring to here are expressions and comments that are way over the top.

Miss Cheerleader is always smiling and tells the world that everything is possible. She never sees the challenges or difficulties associated with a situation. Trust me, in the business world you will be faced with daily challenges and you'll have to be able to communicate the reality of the situation.

One of my current clients is faced with delivering a message that is less than happy. She leads a particular region of the country and, due to market dynamics, last year's inventory massage, and other influential factors, she is probably not going to make her sales target for the quarter. She can pretend that everything is rosy and tell the world she truly believes that she will make the number, or she can step up to the plate and deliver the best plan she knows how, but explain the picture in totality. I have encouraged her to tell the truth and be rooted in data, facts, and trends as she explains her projections. The examples below demonstrate the two ways that this individual could describe this situation. See which way you think is best. And challenge yourself to think back to a time when things weren't so rosy with your business. How did you describe the situation? Were you rooted in solid information? Did you communicate the truth, or what you thought people wanted to hear?

"The current forecast projection reveals that we will not meet 100 percent of the original quarterly sales target. This position is the direct result of market dynamics, competitive activities, and our loading activities from the prior year. The entire team is focused on obtaining incremental promotions that we believe will get us to about the 98 percent level. We are analyzing and examining customized promotional offers that will hit the first of the next quarter. We anticipate that these promotions will allow us to achieve additional volume that will make up for the shortfall experienced this quarter."

"Things have been a little challenging this quarter. The team has really been trying their hardest to reach the sales target. We really want to bring the number home. We know that you are counting on us and we want to come through for you. All hands are on deck! We have faith that we will get there."

Oh, give me a break already! In the second example the person needs to take a reality check. Unfortunately, there are lots of people, especially women, who describe activities around the business in this kind of language. What makes women communicate in this fashion? The answer is that we are afflicted with the People-Pleasing Syndrome. We want the world to like us. Get over it! Business is challenging and as a leader you must be able to communicate the reality of what is happening.

Challenge yourself to become more aware of how you communicate. Think of communication in terms of behaviors, not just words. Spend time conducting a personal evaluation of your efforts. Ask for feedback. If you are conversing with an employee, at the end of the conversation ask the person how clearly you communicated. If you are making a presentation, find an accountability partner to give you candid feedback on how you came across.

> [ . . . knowledge is power only when it is shared and put into action. ]

I want to stress the importance of being transparent in your communication style. I define transparent communication as communication that is rooted in honesty and facts. Don't hold information back. At the risk of repeating myself, knowledge is power only when it is shared and put into action. There are so many people who think that they can hold on to power by not communicating everything. Don't fall victim to this terrible thinking. As you climb the ladder, I plead with you to make open communication a priority.

### Do You Hear What I Hear?

I believe that the most important part of communication is listening. It is the part that is emphasized the least, unfortunately, in most communications training programs. Being a good listener means being fully present in the moment and totally engaged. That means that you are not rehearsing your response in your head or trying to read in between the lines of what is being said. Research shows that we are actively listening only 25 percent of the time; 75 percent of our time is spent on formulating a response.

I cannot tell you how much time is spent in meetings on posturing for position. Half of the time colleagues aren't even listening to each other, and the result is repeated effort and tension. If leaders would focus more on the listening aspect of communications, I believe that we could solve problems more quickly and increase productivity a thousandfold. I have certainly been guilty of not listening and being in the moment. And every time that I have tried to listen in one ear while doing something else, I miss something. How many times have you been talking to someone on the phone and typing an e-mail at the same time? Or reading something while a person is talking to you? We all know how important multitasking is, and women are known for their abilities in this area. But there are times when you must slow down and just listen.

As a leader, getting the information that you need requires you to be a good listener. What is needed is the ability to hear what is being said and to hear what isn't being said. You have to develop the ability to extract the entire story. Following are some tips that will help you to develop your listening skills.

Operate your mouth with a seven-second delay. Think twice about whether you really need to speak before you begin speaking! When people should be listening, most are preparing what they are going to say next. So how can they really be listening? If you delay what you are going to say, maybe you'll find that it doesn't need to be said. Focus on the other person and really be present in the moment.

Know the purpose of your listening. Are you listening to be amiable? To allow someone to fit in? Or to gain knowledge, insight, and understanding? Decide how and what you are listening for before you begin a conversation or a meeting. This step will help you have a purpose for listening in the "right" way.

[ You can't meet the needs of your employees, your customers, your boss, or yourself if you don't listen. ]

Check your listening skills. During a meeting or in a conversation, after you have heard someone speak, you might consider starting your response by saying things like, "What I heard you say was . . . " or "Am I correct when I say that your message was . . . ?"

You can't meet the needs of your employees, your customers, your boss, or yourself if you don't listen. Practice the following listening tips to advance your skills in this area. The most important part of communication for those who are serious about climbing the corporate ladder is a keen ability to listen. Listening requires a lot of energy. The easiest way to lose credibility is to be a poor listener.

### Listening Tips

1. Establish a connection based upon honesty and trust with everyone. Discount any previous reputation that you might have heard about

any person. Be open. No hidden agendas! *Example: Hello, it's nice to meet you. I've heard good things about you. Tell me about your background.*

2. Create clarity of the problem, the situation, and the opportunity. Ask for validation that clarity has been obtained before moving forward. *Example: So we both agree that the problem needing to be resolved is . . .*
3. Demonstrate flexibility and acceptance of the other person's perspective. *Example: I appreciate your point of view, and this is how I think we can combine both of our viewpoints . . .*
4. Create a picture that the person or audience can buy into. *Example: Can you imagine what benefits could be achieved if we were to implement this idea?*
5. Demonstrate logic and reasoning for what you are communicating. *Example: After careful analysis, here are the pros and the cons of the situation . . .*
6. Share your insights on the short- and long-term implications of your message. *Example: If we take this action, it has the following short-term benefits . . . But it also means that from a longer, strategic point of view . . .*
7. Listen and process the response. Be present and in the moment so you can receive the message that is being delivered. *Example: What I hear you saying is . . .*
8. Explain the "why" of what you are communicating. Convey the significance and meaning to the person you are reaching out to. *Example: I'm contacting you about this issue because it impacts your area of responsibility.*
9. Seek to build possibilities out of the feedback you receive, even if the feedback is not positive. *Example: I appreciate what you are saying. I definitely want to take the appropriate action and will take everything that you are sharing into consideration.*
10. Check to make sure that what you are saying is what is actually

being received. *Example: Okay, so far we have identified Problem x. We all agree to the following action steps for the following reasons and benefits . . .*

11. Obtain buy-in for next steps. *Example: Based upon our discussion today, here's what I will take responsibility for and here's what you've agreed to do . . .*

Taking the time to listen to someone else is a choice. Reward your listeners by thanking them for their time and energy. Back before there was e-mail or voice mail, I was a district sales manager transitioning to the position of key account manager. The only way to communicate with others was by phone (and not a cell phone) or in writing—unless you were lucky enough to be able to communicate face to face. I would have to call my sales representatives at home in the evenings to give them their messages. Each of them would receive messages from the distributor or from retailers. I would always end my conversations by saying, "Thank you for your time." On one occasion, I had some friends over for dinner when one of my sales representatives called me. At the end of the conversation, I closed as usual. One of my friends asked me if this person reported to me and I said yes. He then asked me, "If this person reports to you, why are you thanking him for his time?" I hadn't thought that this would seem strange to the outside world. It seemed perfectly natural to me.

> "People aren't going to be interested in listening unless they know you care."

"Thanking someone for their time lets that person know he is valued," I said. Just because someone reports to me doesn't mean he shouldn't be treated with respect. In fact, as the leader, I feel responsible to walk the talk. I feel the need to demonstrate by example. Being the boss doesn't give one permission to speak to people any old way. It should mean the exact opposite. "People aren't going to be interested in listening unless they know you care." These are the words that John F. Kennedy left with us, and they are applicable today, tomorrow, and forever.

## Communicating to Generate Action

As little girls, we were raised to speak when spoken to. If your mother was like mine you heard things like, "Nice girls go last," and "Wait your turn," and "Be seen and not heard." FORGET ALL THOSE OLD TAPES! Let it go, or it will snuff out any chance for you to experience breakthrough success. After I was promoted to the position of vice president and began to attend leadership meetings, I noticed that when I would introduce an idea or a comment that I believed was of value, it would be immediately dismissed. Five minutes later, one of my male colleagues would make the same recommendation that I made. He would reposition it and share it with the group, drawing a reaction that was completely different than the one I received. The idea was now brilliant. At first, I honestly did not know what to do. I thought, "If I bring attention to the fact that I had already made that statement, then the group will think I am too power-hungry and want attention." After repeated experiences where my ideas were stolen with no shame, I decided that I needed to adjust my communication skills to better manage the situation. The communication behavior modifications that I made empowered me and enabled me to earn the reputation of a value-adding leader. Let me share six communication behavior-improvement steps that I think will help you come across as more informed and more powerful.

- STATE YOUR COMMENTS WITH BOLDNESS: Avoid using words like "I think." Instead, use words that convey confidence, such as "The research shows . . . " or "My experience suggests . . . "
- BE CONCISE: Don't go on and on. You're not delivering the news—just making a point.
- PICK THE RIGHT TIME TO SPEAK: Don't get drowned out by trying to force a comment when everyone else is speaking. Pick the right moment to introduce your thoughts. Start by saying something like, "After listening to your thoughts (or opinions), let me share a different perspective . . . "
- WATCH YOUR BODY LANGUAGE: It's truly a good thing to express yourself with your entire body. But in the boardroom, controlled motions are much better received than flailing arms and legs.
- BE QUICK TO RECLAIM YOUR IDEAS: If your idea or comment is not acknowledged and is then introduced by someone else, reclaim your voice. After the person repeats what you have just said, quickly thank her for listening and remind the group that you introduced the same thought earlier. Say something like, "Obviously you were listening earlier when I made the same comment. Let me restate my position and see if we share the same opinion on this issue." I promise you that this person will not be so quick to steal your thoughts the next time.
- OPEN YOUR MOUTH: Not being heard is simply not acceptable. A soft-spoken voice will destroy your credibility. You don't need a bullhorn, but you do need to speak with depth and volume.

The tips listed above will make you a more effective listener and therefore a more effective communicator. I cannot stress enough the importance of developing your skills in this area.

The other area of communication I want to emphasize is the need to communicate in a way that gets others to act. As you advance within the business world, it will become abundantly clear that communicating a vision is critical. I suspect you will discover that in today's marketplace, collaboration is essential. Collaboration, in my opinion, is the real smoking gun that helps organizations take their overall performance to the next level. Collaboration is a natural strength for women. We must leverage this talent for all that it is worth. Will it be hard? Yes, it will take a lot more than a notion to help people move from a top-down mentality to a collaborative one. But it is absolutely essential. How can you be effective in creating action through use of words? ASK. Get in the habit of asking people for their commitment to honor your requests. Then make sure that they understand the timeline and have the resources needed to execute. So many people make the mistake of not asking. Effective communication includes getting the buy-in for what you are saying. But in order to get the buy-in for your vision or project, or to stimulate others to take action, communication has got to explain the Who, What, and Why.

[ Collaboration . . . is the real smoking gun that helps organizations take their overall performance to the next level. ]

One of my clients is going through an acquisition. During the early integration of the two companies, the senior executive team left messages for the entire company on a weekly basis. Once the initial phase of the integration was complete, the communication dried up completely. Employees felt lost and in the dark. What happened when senior executives didn't communicate effectively? Rather than focusing on integrating the two companies, finding synergies, and increasing productivity, the employees began to focus on exchanging their opinions about what was going to happen. People made up their own stories of what they thought was going on in the company. Most often the stories that are made up don't reflect the real business situation. Negative thoughts passed through the organization like wildfire. The end result was extremely negative and could have totally been avoided with proper communication.

Communication is essential for career success. This is an area that will always need refining, so develop a plan to enhance continuous growth.

## Points Worth Remembering

- Effective communication builds connection and leads to empowerment.
- Think of communication in terms of behaviors, not just words.
- The most important element of communication is listening.
- Leaders must communicate often and answer the Who, What, and Why questions to get buy-in and create action.
- Practice open and transparent communication.

# 7

# MARKETING THE BRAND CALLED YOU

*"Your Personal Brand is the ultimate currency, because it determines to what extent others—from your superiors to your spouse—listen to you and give weight to what you say."*

—Peter Montoya

## YOUR PERSONAL VALUE PROPOSITION

You are the product. Without an effective marketing plan to get you noticed, respected, and sought after, your climb won't be successful. There are many ways to go about marketing yourself. In a work environment that is in constant change, personal marketing is critical to your success. I would suggest that it is through personal marketing that you establish yourself as a leader.

It's important to understand that marketing yourself is not about putting on an act. It's about being natural and reflecting the best you can offer. Just one cautionary note: *Make sure you are ready. It takes a short amount of time to develop a reputation; it takes forever to undo a reputation.* You can't afford mistakes in your marketing execution. Often the first impression is the only impression you get to make. I recently heard someone say, "You are either in the market to get a new job or to keep the job that you already have." Either way, you have got to have the mind-set that someone is always watching and evaluating. The hard work you have done to address your strengths and weaknesses is about to pay off.

[ "You are either in the market to get a new job or to keep the job that you already have." ]

Marketing yourself is not about stepping on others or becoming a "yes" person. It is about adding value and letting the world know about the value you are adding. It takes courage to be able to remain authentic to your beliefs and values while climbing the career ladder. One of the most difficult challenges you will face as you take on increasing responsibility is to allow your actions to be guided by your beliefs, not by the popular vote.

One of the many reasons why people are unsuccessful within an organization is because they don't understand what I call the "value relationship." The value relationship is the connection between the work that you do and the company's bottom line. Another reason is because they don't enjoy what they do and perhaps they don't enjoy the culture or the environment in which they work. We have dealt with techniques that will help you identify the kind of work that aligns with your goals and values. Now we need to ensure that you understand how your role fits into the organization. This is the essence of the Value Proposition. For you to succeed in any organization there are several key questions that you must be able to answer and understand!

1. What is the mission statement or the number one goal of the organization?

___________________________________________

___________________________________________

___________________________________________

___________________________________________

2. How does your role contribute to the achievement of this goal?

___________________________________________

___________________________________________

___________________________________________

___________________________________________

3. What are the values of the organization?

___________________________________________

___________________________________________

___________________________________________

___________________________________________

4. What are the core competencies of your department?

___________________________________________

___________________________________________

___________________________________________

___________________________________________

5. What value does your department contribute to the achievement of the organization?

___________________________________________

___________________________________________

___________________________________________

___________________________________________

You must be able to explain how your function adds value to the execution of the company's goals and objectives. Every role in the organization is valuable to the execution of the strategy. Making your connection to the big picture will enable you to market yourself with power and confidence.

Let's turn now to how you can add value to your current position.

- Identify the top three critical needs within your department.

1. ______________________________
2. ______________________________
3. ______________________________

- Identify one way that you can make a major contribution to improve one of the areas listed above.

______________________________

______________________________

______________________________

______________________________

- Using the work that you have already done, develop a goal and outline the appropriate steps and timeline to implement your plan.

______________________________

______________________________

______________________________

______________________________

______________________________

______________________________

______________________________

______________________________

Ask for an assignment that increases your understanding of the multiple roles within your department. Focus on obtaining an assignment that stretches your areas of development. Defer assignments that add no value to your skill package.

Volunteer to do work after hours in other departments where you may not otherwise gain exposure. Building on your current competencies helps you to engage in a value relationship that grows in level of executive awareness and importance to the execution of the organization's strategy.

## SUCCESSFULLY MARKETING YOUR PERSONAL BRAND

Building your career requires that you establish the brand called you—"YOU, Inc." if you will. Your brand is based on your strengths, talents, beliefs, values, and vision. There is something about each item you purchase at the mall or grocery story that motivates you to select it. It may be the price. It may be the packaging. It may be the latest research about the benefits of the product. Or it may be that the advertising has worked and you want to try the brand for the first time. Something triggers your purchase activity. It's the same with you as a brand.

> The best-kept secrets are just that—secrets. You've got to market your brand.

In order for the organization to want to promote you, there must be something about you that is different. Your brand must scream quality, substance, and results. It's not enough for you to understand what your brand stands for. The best-kept secrets are just that—secrets. You've got to market your brand.

Lisa is a good example of the power of building and marketing a brand. Lisa is a polished, developing professional. She works for a large manufacturing company and holds the position of regional manager. This is a field position, and as a result, she has limited interaction with the senior executives who are in the home office.

Lisa had a desire to be promoted into the home office. She had a very supportive boss who wanted to help her achieve her career goals. She decided that what was needed in her plan was a marketing campaign. She wanted to get the word out about her ideas and decided the best way to do that was to share her ideas with her counterparts first. She offered to visit with each region and bring a few people to help demonstrate the value of the procedures the team had established to better manage inventory.

She decided that it would be good to invite some of the right people from the home office to the next presentation. She gained the support of her boss. He extended the invitation to his counterparts and to a couple of senior executives from the business development department.

Lisa made a great presentation. She marketed herself and her team. She came across as strong, confident, and smart. Everyone was impressed. Less than six months later, Lisa was assigned to two strategic projects focused on designing new ways to address the market. This is a classic example of marketing your brand. Lisa didn't wait for the opportunity to come to her. She created the opportunity!

Compare this scenario to Tony. Tony works for the same company as Lisa. He works in the customer service department, but he has a strong desire to work in the marketing department. He is perfect to work in the marketing department because he is in the target segment that the company's products need to appeal to. He has not shared his ideas with very many people. He feels that his position as a customer service representative places him so low on the totem pole that he would not be viewed as worthy of interacting with senior management. Tony lacks the confidence to take matters into his own hands. It has been more than six months and nothing has happened. Why? The brand called Tony is solid, enthusiastic, and connected to the right consumer segment. So what's missing? Why hasn't he made a career move? Tony lacks the confidence to take matters into his own hands. The right people simply don't know anything about him.

Tony is well positioned. The very people he wants to work with surround him. He sees the senior executive passing in the halls. He has every chance in the world to market himself, but he doesn't. Tony is convinced that his manager will help him achieve his goals. His manager, although willing to help, doesn't have the power and presence within the company to get Tony the attention he needs to promote the value he could add to the marketing efforts of the company.

Don't ever give your marketing power or responsibility to anyone else. You are your best agent! No one can express your passion, drive, and commitment like you can. Any support that you can get from your manager or anyone else should be extra. If you want to see your career flourish, design your own marketing plan. Don't wait for the opportunity to come to you. Do as Lisa did—create it!

The following seven points will assist you in developing your personal brand.

1. AUTHENTICITY—Being authentic occurs when you are living in integrity. It is rooted in your values and beliefs. Once you understand how you can add value using your talents, skills, beliefs, and values, then you open the door to establishing yourself as a brand.
2. CONSISTENCY/RELIABILITY—Once your brand is established, you must be consistent. Others will begin to expect you to act a certain way. If you have positioned your brand as "high quality," then you must constantly deliver based on that brand reputation.
3. ALLURE—A great brand has something that is important to others. There is something unique and special about what you bring to the table. Get in touch with your point of difference and your brand will shine.
4. VALUE—A great brand has value and is therefore treasured. The value never goes away. It only gets better with time. Your value allows you to serve and sow seeds that reap great harvests over and over again.
5. FLEXIBILITY—A great brand knows how to reach diverse audiences. Its flexibility enables a connection to be made at multiple levels.
6. CHARACTER—A great brand is rooted in strong moral conviction and is not afraid to set boundaries to remain true to convictions.
7. VISION—A growing brand is always looking for new ways to stretch, to move forward, and to learn.

These seven features of a brand must be connected to your core competencies. Later on in this chapter, several examples are provided to help you understand how to tie it all together.

## SHARING THE BRAND CALLED YOU

Once you have clarity about your brand, you can begin to develop a communication strategy that helps you share it. The following questions are designed to help you take action to market yourself. Answering these questions will help you develop your communication plan. It will also help you identify what internal or external resources you should seek out to enhance your brand.

What actions will I take to immediately, positively impact my brand in the next 30 days?

________________________________________

________________________________________

________________________________________

________________________________________

________________________________________

How and with whom will I share my intention? (Make a bold declaration.)

________________________________________

________________________________________

________________________________________

________________________________________

________________________________________

What resources do I need to use to support my brand? (Trade magazines, a written plan, training, coaching, etc.)

________________________________________

________________________________________

________________________________________

________________________________________

________________________________________

Whom can I count on to check the authenticity of how I deliver my brand?

________________________________________

________________________________________

________________________________________

________________________________________

________________________________________

## Work It!

In order to experience success in marketing yourself, I believe that you must have a spirit of service. You must be willing to find a way to use your talents to serve other people. It is then and only then that others will help you achieve your goals. Your approach should include three steps.

Step 1: Fine-tune your personal commercial. You got your first glimpse of a personal commercial in chapter 3. Here are several additional examples. These examples build on the work that you did in chapter 3. Armed with that knowledge, now it's time to craft and practice your own commercial.

Following are three examples of personal commercials, sometimes called "elevator speeches" because of their brevity.

"I am a corporate lawyer specializing in employee relations. I have significant expertise in proactive counseling, and coaching senior executives in addressing employee problems, business initiatives, and employee relations strategies."

"I am a dynamic business development manager who adds value to the organization by developing new territory. I have a keen ability to read trends and convert my understanding of the trends into business-building opportunities for the company."

"I am a performance enhancement expert who specializes in developing strategies and solutions that bring out the best performance in individuals and corporations."

Use the following guide to develop your own personal commercial.

- Who are you?
- What is your area of expertise? Explain what that means.
- How does your expertise add value to the organization?

STEP 2: Ensure that you understand the audience you are talking to. You don't want to come across as cocky or stiff! Take the time to become familiar with the background and goals of the people that you will be marketing to. Look for ways that you can connect with them. As an example, perhaps you attended the same college. Or maybe you knew someone who went to the same college. Look for any angle that allows you to connect with the person, not the professional.

STEP 3: Create opportunities to market yourself.

- Request special assignments.
- Write articles for the company newsletter.
- Create a company newsletter.
- Volunteer to train a new employee.
- Write a training program outline (it helps to tie this effort to your own goals and aspirations—it makes you look like the expert!).
- Get on a task force.
- Talk to people at every level within the organization—you never know who is connected to whom. Don't underestimate the power of "word-of-mouth" marketing.
- Network at every level.
- A little secret: Secretaries are the best allies you can have. They have the ear of the person you want to get to.
- Develop good listening skills. Often you'll discover opportunities that have yet to make it onto the grapevine.

## ASK AND YOU SHALL RECEIVE

One of the most important lessons I learned on my way to the top was this: *If you don't ask, you won't receive.* It's not just marketing yourself that will get you the career of your dreams; you must be willing to expose your passion by asking for exactly what you want. As an example, in my corporate experience there was an unwritten rule that before a person could become a section sales manager, he or she had to spend time in the home office. I wanted to be promoted to the section sales manager position, but I was not ready to go into the home office. I also knew that I would have to be strategic in expressing my desire to remain in Los Angeles while emphasizing my strong belief that I could be the "new model" for leadership development by receiving a promotion without having spent time in the home office. As fate would have it, the senior vice president was coming to Los Angeles for a field visit. Opportunity!!!!

I hosted his visit and was able to spend a considerable amount of one-on-one time with this gentleman. It was during this time that I offered him insight on the workforce trends. I was particularly focused on helping him to understand that not everyone can move in order to advance his or her career. I went on to explain the many benefits the company could derive by exploring new ways to expose employees with "high potential," without having to move them to the home office. Notice that I was careful to sell the idea before I began to sell myself.

> Don't wait for the opportunity to present itself to you. Create the opportunity and then ask for what you want!

I further positioned this dialogue from a strategic-thinking leadership position. After all, I wasn't just talking about the benefits for me; I was talking about the benefits and opportunities for the company. My point is this: If I had just accepted the standard and not ventured out to ask about new possibilities, I might not have received that next promotion. I'm happy to say that it was only two months later that I received a promotion to the section sales manager position. I know deep inside that had I not been willing to step out of the box and introduce a new thinking process and ask for support, it wouldn't have happened.

Don't wait for the opportunity to present itself to you. Create the opportunity and then ask for what you want!

## Points Worth Remembering

- It is through personal marketing that you establish yourself as a leader.
- Your brand is based upon your strengths, talents, beliefs, values, and vision.
- Don't wait for opportunities for exposure to come to you—create them!
- Developing a personal commercial enables you to speak with confidence and conviction about what you bring to the table.
- Marketing yourself in a spirit of service to others enables you to build powerful connections that lead to breakthrough performance.

# RELATIONSHIPS: THE MISSING LINK

*"The most important ingredient we put into any relationship is not what we say or what we do, but what we are."*
—Peter Montoya

## THE IMPORTANCE OF RELATIONSHIPS

In today's turbulent market, change is expected. There are no job guarantees, not for anyone. What does that mean for you? It means you must stay on top of your game. You must focus on understanding the trends, acquiring the skills needed to successfully manage change, and be on purpose in pursuing your goals. Besides understanding your strengths and weaknesses and being able to develop an action plan that supports achievement of your career goals, you also need to focus on building strong relationships. Building strong business relationships is just as important as acquiring skills.

[Building strong business relationships is just as important as acquiring skills.]

The relationships that you build should be based upon trust and authenticity. It is not about befriending someone to use them. It is about giving and getting. Business relationships aren't a whole lot different from personal relationships. Truth be told, we probably spend more time with our business associates than we do with those in our personal lives. Relationships require open communication, energy, and nourishment.

I have a friend, Pamela, who is a master at building relationships. She is better than anyone else I have ever seen. What's her secret? I recently asked her about what she has done to build so many relationships with senior executives throughout the country. Her answers are worth sharing. She gave me five critical elements:

1. Connect with people who have common values and principles.
2. Be willing to give and to help.
3. Quickly get away and stay away from people who suck your energy.
4. Always follow up (notes, letters, cards, phone calls).
5. Know yourself.

Pretty good advice, don't you think? Stop now and make up your own list of the critical success factors in building effective relationships. Refer to this list and make notes as you read the rest of this chapter. By the end of the chapter you'll know exactly what you need to do to develop your own relationship strategy.

## A Real Reality Check

It's unfortunate but true—there are snipers in every organization. Snipers are usually egotistical and are only willing to endorse an idea if it's their idea and no one else gets the credit. It's also unfortunate that, generally speaking, they are high enough in power to do lots of damage. There is no way to avoid these types of individuals. They exist at every company—except those companies where hidden agendas are not tolerated (and perhaps those companies that are smart enough to tie a certain percentage of compensation to performance as a whole). This is why it is critical to have senior champions for your ideas. These are people who believe in you! These are people who want to see you succeed and are willing to help you. There is one caution that I will share on this subject: *Never align yourself with only one champion or sponsor in a company.* Why? If that one person decides to leave, your anchor disappears.

The following scenario happened to one of my clients. She was a mid-level manager who had been hired by the then senior vice president of sales. She had been brought in from another company. She was well thought of and respected for her intelligence. She was, to some degree, successful. Unfortunately, she focused all her efforts on the relationship with the one person who brought her into the company. She would use his name to advance her projects or to get special provisions to participate in programs that employees at her level normally wouldn't participate in. Some of the employees at her level and above, who weren't receiving the same kind of benefits she was, resented her, despite the fact that she was really good at what she did. About a year after she joined the company, the senior vice president who hired her left the company. With his exit she no longer had any support. She floundered to connect with the same people whom she had belittled, and they rejected her. She had to start from ground zero. In fact, she was starting in the negative because of all the damage that she had done. She now understands the value of building relationships throughout the organization. She acknowledges that while a name can get you in the door to build a relationship, ultimately the relationship is based upon what *you* bring to the table.

What I recommend to you is that you find champions at every level of the organization. I also recommend that these champions be cross-functional. Find at least one champion in your current discipline, but the rest should be from other areas that you have or need to get experience in. Champions should be in strategic positions throughout the organization so that they can be your eyes and ears in situations or discussions you are not necessarily privy to.

Use the strength of your champions to help you introduce new ideas, concepts, or initiatives to the organization. And be sure to keep your ideas rooted in a profit-benefit analysis for the company. In other words, don't selfishly serve up an idea just to get promoted. Serve it up from a leadership position. For example, Paul knows that his company is behind in adopting technology that will allow the organization to get a better handle on the level of financial exposure that comes as a result of checks written at the local field sales level. He also knows that the company does not want to change anything until the entire accounting system can be revamped. How should he go about selling his idea? First, he should do his homework. He needs to find out how much money has actually been lost and how much is at risk. He then needs to find a senior leader who is influential and open to hearing the case for moving forward with the project now versus later. He must be thorough in researching companies that can provide the services his organization needs. He must also take the time to find out what those needs are, internally and externally. Sound like a lot of work? It is!

That's why there is power in linking up with individuals in the organization who share your ideas.

Navigating for success is not about doing it alone. In fact, quite the opposite is true. It is about connecting and leveraging the relationships you have and the relationships of those who are linked to you. Paul was able to use his champions to merchandise his ideas for him and with him.

In the next chapter we'll review the importance of creating a strong network or support group. For now, just remember that whether your objective is to sell new technology software or to start a day care center, as the executive mentioned earlier did, you must do your homework. You must connect with others. You must find senior champions. And you must have a profit-benefit proposal.

Use the next exercise to help you understand what to look for to enhance your ability to navigate the landscape. You might also consider taking this opportunity to set up a Personal Feedback Loop to assist your development in this area.

- Who are the up-and-coming stars in the organization?
- How are these stars connected to the senior leadership of the organization?
- What do you know about the desires of those who are in executive positions at the company? (Do they have families? Does each of them want to become the next CEO?)
- What are their perspectives on work and life?
- How do members of the executive committee interface with each other? Do they find a way to reach a point of compromise on major issues, or are they engaged in petty disputes that halt progress?
- What wakes the senior team up at night? What are they most concerned about, regarding the business?
- Do employees get together for after-hours functions or sports functions?

- Do the senior leaders invite employee challenges?
- Are people promoted as a result of hard work and value-added contributions, or are they promoted based on the way they look?
- Do you consistently demonstrate your ability to influence others without stepping on others' toes?

## The Art of Powerful Connections

How do you pull all of this together? It's the power of harnessing relationships! I can't tell you how many of my clients come to me with great business acumen, good articulation, and tremendous presentation skills, but without people connections. You can't get so busy in your climb that you forget about the value of people. Some of the first questions I ask my clients are, "Who are your champions? Who are your sponsors? What kind of relationships do you have with people throughout the organization?" If I asked you right now to name five people at a senior level within your organization that you know and have a relationship with, what would your response be? And if I went on to ask you for the names of another five people at senior levels outside of your organization, what would you say then? If you can't answer these two questions with ease, then you need to work on building these relationships.

It takes so much more than getting the results to navigate the maze of a corporate environment. Do you remember when I said in the introduction that you will get your energy from people? It's true. It is the people connection that gives you the cause to strive for, and that encourages you to sell the goal that gets accomplished and makes a difference!

[ It is the people connection that gives you the cause to strive for, and that encourages you to sell the goal that gets accomplished and makes a difference! ]

Employees want relationships with their leaders. One way you can advance your career aspirations is to always conduct yourself based upon the values and beliefs that we talked about in the first chapter. Beyond that, you can be open to formulating authentic relationships that are based on trust and honesty. This means no hidden agendas. No surprises. And it means that you will have to be consistent. In other words, you can't be friends only when it is convenient for your career.

Building powerful connections cannot be faked. You must be genuine. People can read through someone who wants to schmooze for self-serving reasons in a flash. Recently, a client told me that one of her mentors had encouraged her to stop trying to get on the senior executives' calendars because it looked as if she was on a political mission. She is a mid-level manager who has aspirations of becoming a vice president. She is assertive, and that is her normal personality inside and outside of work. She is one who sees what she wants and goes straight after it. After taking the hard feedback, she asked me about it. I asked her to describe how she had gone about connecting with the senior leaders that she wanted to meet. She said that she simply pulled up their calendars on the computer system and placed herself on their agendas. "Oh my!" I said. That is not a good way to get to know someone. And no wonder it looked a little different and self-serving to the outside world. Sometimes we have to be willing to take the scenic route instead of the direct path to get where we want to go. This kind of style flexing is critical the higher you go up the ladder.

I suggested that she first focus on building a bridge, using her existing network to get to these individuals. She could identify one or two people who could facilitate an introduction for her. She also needed a reason to go and meet with these people. Just dropping by to introduce yourself is not a good way to build relationships. You have to demonstrate your character and how much you care in order for relationships to develop. It takes trust. Building trusting relationships requires energy, time, and effort. She was in such a rush to schmooze that she forgot to take care of the foundational elements of building a relationship.

## People Connect with Leaders, Not Organizations

A 2002 Watson Wyatt survey of nearly 13,000 workers found that worker trust and confidence in senior management fell during 2000–2002. It suggests that, unless reversed, this presents a major threat to future corporate competitiveness. Speaking on behalf of the company, Ilene Gochman, Watson Wyatt's national practice leader, said, "Unless corporate America can resolve the crisis of confidence among its employees, it has little hope of restoring the trust and confidence of investors that is crucial in these economic times."

Research shows, without question, that in corporations where high levels of trust exist, returns to the shareholders are significantly higher. This graphic illustration depicts the three critical components of building a relationship.

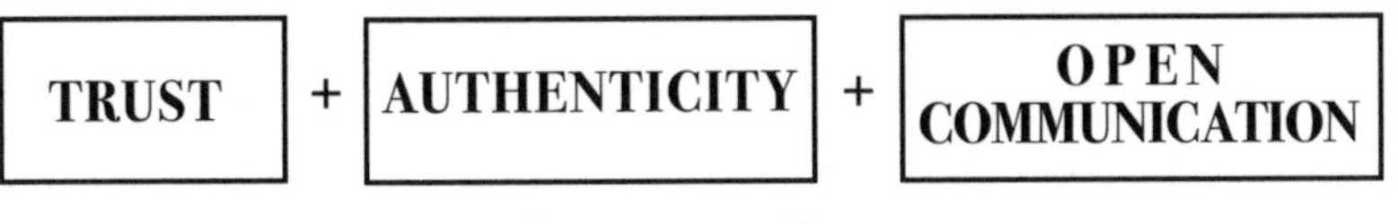


= REAL AND LASTING RELATIONSHIPS

To really connect with an individual, he or she has to see you as a "whole" person. It used to be that expressing emotional caring from one employee to another was viewed as negative. That is so old school. No one, no matter who they are or on what level they serve, can check the emotional part of their personality at the door. Your emotions are critical components that make you who you are. We are humans, and we are wired to make emotional connections. We truly want to belong.

[ We are humans, and we are wired to make emotional connections. ]

A company that is an excellent example of building a culture where caring is valued is The Container Store. In a *Fortune* article where The Container Store employees were interviewed, 97 percent of the participants said that the reason why people love to work at The Container Store was because "people care about each other here." Tindell and Garrett Boone, the founders, realized early on that they had to do more than pay lip service when it came to valuing their employees. It's the same concept with building relationships one on one. People want to feel valued.

The following statement was made by Tom Sanders,

CEO of Yahoo!, as quoted in *Fast Company:* "The secret to being a high-impact leader: Learn as much as you can as quickly as you can and share your knowledge aggressively; expand your network of people who share your values, and connect as many of them with each other as possible." At the core of building a successful career is the power that comes from relationships. Relationships are developed and maintained based upon three principles: trust, communication, and consistent performance. Trust is earned, not given. It is through our ability to trust that we are able to develop faith in someone else. The element of trust has taken on a whole new level of importance in the corporate environment.

> [ It takes self-leadership, commitment, and emotional effort to let go of perceptions, miscommunications, misunderstandings, and mishaps that damage our connections. ]

At the core of any relationship is the ability to make an emotional connection. The influence of emotions has been a much-debated topic. Daniel Goleman really brought this to the forefront in his book *Emotional Intelligence.* In this book, Goleman makes the case that emotional intelligence counts more than IQ or expertise for determining who excels at a job. I encourage all my clients to read this book. And I encourage them to practice making behavior modifications that enhance what I call emotional discipline.

Emotional discipline is so important for women. We have a reputation for being too emotional. This gives the senior executives who can help to advance our careers the impression that we aren't capable of handling difficult situations without becoming overly emotional. The essence of emotional intelligence is found in three key elements: 1) understanding your own emotions and how to adjust or discipline them appropriately, 2) understanding how your emotions impact those around you, and 3) assessing your ability to mature emotionally.

It takes self-leadership, commitment, and emotional effort to let go of perceptions, miscommunications, misunderstandings, and mishaps that damage our connections. The truth of the matter is that every day we are faced with this challenge and provided with the option to transform and build a new future. Relationships cannot be sustained without open, honest communication. People can get comfortable with you if you are prepared to lead with vulnerability. A person who leads with vulnerability is often unaware about being comfortable.

Most people trying to climb the ladder view vulnerability as a sign of underdevelopment or weakness. This is not the case. Let me explain in more detail. When you first meet someone, if they act as though they are perfect or know everything better than you, what do you think? You think "What a creep," don't you? Yet that is exactly what a lot of people do. Why? They are trying to prove themselves. To build effective business relationships, get rid of any insecurity that drives you to pretend you are better than anyone else. Focus on developing a style that allows people to be comfortable around you.

### Confidence Breeds Self-Esteem

What I have found in my last two years of coaching combined with my eighteen years of cross-functional business experience is that people in the business environment shy away from building relationships. Not because they don't believe in the value of relationships, but because they lack self-confidence. This lack of self-confidence makes them unwilling to open themselves up.

This belief was confirmed during a recent coaching call. The individual I was speaking with is a warm and caring person who has consistently achieved success. He has, in recent years, reached a plateau. People sometimes refer to him as being aloof and hard to get to know. He wants to advance within the organization, but, as he puts it, "I don't know if it is worth it to build the relationships needed to help me achieve my goals. I'm just not willing to open myself up."

> A company that wants productive and happy employees will find a way to break from the old school thought that feelings and emotions need to be checked at the door.

After a lot of probing, he admitted that it was because he didn't want people to find out that he wasn't as smart as he wanted them to believe he was. And he didn't want to invest in the relationships only to be hurt. It was safer for him to keep people at a distance than to open himself up. I don't believe that there is any way you can experience true success without opening yourself up. I think that God wired us to connect with others. And I believe that this will come to light more than ever in the twenty-first century. Why? Because companies are finally realizing that, at the end of the day, it's about people. It's about connections. An organization can't treat its employees any old way and then expect them to be loyal. A company that wants productive and happy employees will find a way to break from the old school thought that feelings and emotions need to be checked at the door.

In *Primal Leadership,* Daniel Goleman talks at length about the power of emotional connections that are made between individuals. He and the other authors, Richard Boyatzis and Annie McKee, suggest that the manner in which leaders act—not just what they do, but how they do it—is a fundamental key to effective leadership. He also says that when people feel good, they work at their best. I know this to be true from real-life experience.

Sheila is a brilliant woman. She loves data like some people love football. She is absolutely turned on by data. Her career climb took her through several companies. She had been with her (and my) current company for about eight years. I watched her from afar. She was tall, beautiful, and smart. (What a great combination!) She worked in the market research department, and her responsibilities included not just gathering data but also translating it into meaningful information that would help the senior executive team make good decisions. As a result of the many presentations she made, she was often in front of me and my peers. But we would frequently have to ask her to speak up or repeat herself because she spoke so softly.

It was obvious to me that her confidence was low. What wasn't obvious to me was why. She seemed to have all the pieces of the puzzle. As fate would have it, an opening came up in my department that required her exact area of expertise. It was suggested to me that I interview her, and I did. It was during that interview that I discovered Sheila felt used and not valued. I shared my philosophy of developing my team and my sincere commitment to helping each member reach his or her professional goals. When she heard that, she lit up. She experienced an actual physical transformation. "That would be a totally different environment to work in," she said. "I might really feel appreciated."

"You are valuable," I said. "You are critical to the business. Your ideas are great, and I want you to open up your heart and enjoy working for the company."

She admitted that she had kept to herself because she had been so belittled by her previous manager that she found herself retreating rather than growing. Curiosity soon got the best of me and I asked her to describe her current environment. She shared with me how her boss would take her ideas and claim them as his own. He would take her presentations and present them as if he had done the work. He would reprimand her for stopping by senior executives' offices without an appointment to discuss her marketing ideas.

> [ You must be comfortable with who you are and what your value is in order to have the confidence to take on the world. ]

All of these terrible experiences had lessened her confidence. The net impact was an employee who was unhappy and certainly not as productive as she could have been. Just hearing that someone found her to be valuable and was willing to give her the exposure to demonstrate her skills sent a bolt of energy to her soul. That soft-spoken woman began to roar, and so did her career!

What's the point here? Simply this: *You must be comfortable with who you are and what your value is in order to have the confidence to take on the world.* There's no reason to allow someone else to make you feel less than valued. You are in charge of your own feelings. Also, there is no reason to let someone else take your work and get credit for it. Speak up! Here are several tips I suggest you think about to protect your ideas from being borrowed without permission.

1. Share your concepts and beliefs with a wider audience than just your boss. Ask for input and feedback.
2. Send out a pre-session teaser with nuggets of the research or concepts that you will be using to support your position. People will appreciate being kept in the loop if the information is concise and value-added.
3. Conduct face-to-face debriefings after you make a presentation. Use this opportunity to reinforce your hard work.
4. Build good relationships with senior executives at your boss's level and above. Spend time cultivating the relationships, sharing information, and building awareness for the projects you are working on.
5. Approach the credit taker directly but in a spirit of sincerity. Find out why he would present your work as his own. Ask him if he needs help. Keep this person as an ally instead of creating an enemy.

I recently hosted a workshop where a really good friend of mine talked about the necessity of being comfortable in your own skin. I like to describe it as "likeable confidence." It's when you know that you are good and you don't have to make a fuss about it to let the world know you are good. I don't know where along the way I adopted the philosophy that when you are really good the world markets for you. You don't have to say very much for yourself. You must make connections and you must market your accomplishments, but you don't have to pretend that you know it all! Nobody knows it all.

As Franklin Covey describes in his book *Seven Habits of Highly Successful People,* trust is built and maintained based on an emotional bank account. The Bank Account Theory suggests that when you do something positive that adds value to a relationship, you make a positive deposit. On the flip side of the coin, if you do something that is negative or damaging to the relationship, you receive a debit or withdrawal. This is why it is so important to build a solid reputation as part of your strategy for a successful career. You need to constantly make deposits in every single relationship.

## Points Worth Remembering

- Building relationships is as important as building skills and competencies.
- Relationships require open communication, energy, and nourishment.
- Use your sponsors and champions to help you introduce new concepts to the organization.
- Trust + Authenticity + Open Communication = Real and Lasting Relationships
- Not just what you do but how you do it is critical for effective leadership.

# It Takes a Community of Resources

*"Resources are everywhere; all you have to do is ask for help."*

—Author Unknown

## Resources: Helping You Achieve Success

A well-thought-out career plan includes identification and use of any and all available resources, both internal and external to your company. The more diverse the resources, the richer the information and experience you'll gather. You'll find that there is such a plethora of information, you'll have to prioritize the data in terms of what lends the most value to your objectives. You must focus on extracting from these resources the skills, insights, and perspectives that help you to broaden your competency base and leadership effectiveness.

Here's a list of options for your consideration:

- Internal/external training programs
- The local library
- Books
- Videos
- The Internet

- Newspapers
- Industry publications
- A buddy to brainstorm ideas with
- Your church
- The local chamber of commerce
- Industry associations
- Local universities
- Alumni programs
- Career fairs
- Sponsors
- Mentors

## Specific Internet Resources

Career Fairs: www.careerfairs.com
Overall Career Service Center: www.jobsmart.org
Goal Setting: www.topachievement.com
Professional Journals www.ecola.com
Forums: www.n2h2.com/KOVACS/
Assessment Tests: www.kingdomality.com
Professional Associations: www.ipl.org/ref/AON/
Trends: www.businessweek.com
Company Information: www.hoovers.com
Work/Life Balance: www.workfamily.com and www.bluitsuit.com
www.catalyst.com
www.networkofexecutivewomen.com

## Newspapers/Magazines

*The Wall Street Journal*
*USA Today*

*Fast Company* magazine
*Harvard Business Review*
*Forum*
Industry publications

A close friend of mine starts her day every day by reading *The Wall Street Journal* front to back. She finds that the information contained in the articles and the insights on recent developments and trends in the business world enable her to present herself in a better light. It works for her. Finds something that works for you!

Another step you might consider is to set up a personal board of directors. A personal board of directors is a group of people that you have selected to be your advisors. This team of people should be carefully selected, based upon their character, values, principles, and experience. These are the people who you can call on to ask questions and get advice. Developing a personal board of directors takes time. And it takes commitment from the people who serve in this capacity for you. Take your time to select these people and then make sure you explain what you need from them and ask for their commitment in serving as trusted advisors.

Yet another option is to form a Mastermind Group. Mastermind Groups are composed of people who want to learn from each other. These groups can be as small as six people or as large as twenty people. They normally meet on a monthly basis. The purpose of the meetings is to discuss success stories or problems and to deal with any questions. If you're reading this thinking you don't have enough time to keep up with all of this, formulate a Mastermind Group and spread the work. Here's how you get started:

STEP 1: Identify a list of people that you think would like to participate in the group and would benefit from participating.

STEP 2: Write a brief script that details the purpose of the group. Make sure to cover the following:

- How much time the person will need to commit.
- How much work will be involved.
- How often you will meet.
- Where you will meet.
- Who else you are asking to participate.

STEP 3: Develop a list of potential books to review, topics to cover, and issues that might be of interest.

STEP 4: Obtain commitment from participants.

STEP 5: Hold a kickoff meeting (share the list of potential areas of focus—see Step 3).

STEP 6: Get started!

Honestly, it's that easy to get a Mastermind Group going. The hard part is getting everyone to place the time commitment to the group on their priority list. If the topics are timely and value-added, the interest will remain.

During the course of your career, you'll find all kinds of resources. I encourage you to start a resource file or book. You never know when you are going to need this information. So keep it handy in a place where you can put your fingers on it at a moment's notice. Keep all your contact names and information in this area too. This is also a great place to file articles that may be valuable for future reference.

## The Role of a Mentor

A mentor is defined by Webster as a person looked upon for wise advice and counsel. At some point during your journey in building your career, you will need a good mentor. It needs to happen sooner rather than later. In fact, if you don't have a formal mentor, set an objective to find one within the next thirty days. A mentor can play a key role in your ongoing learning and development. In an article written by Couillart and Kelly, the importance of mentoring and learning was put this way: "Learning builds self-esteem and promotes competence and efficacy in approaching work-related problems." The more self-knowledge an employee acquires, the more he or she can contribute to an organization. Mentoring, therefore, is a win-win for the company that you work for and for your own development.

My husband used to play the role of a mentor when I was in corporate, since there weren't any mentoring relationships available to me. I used to say to him that he was good at helping me make a well-needed attitude adjustment. He was able to get me to see situations in a completely different light. My husband is about four years older than me, and he has a little more experience than I do. But more importantly, he has the bird's-eye view. He can see the big picture. The big picture includes things that you can't see because you are in the middle of it. You know the old saying—you can't see the forest for the trees.

Selecting a mentor is a very personal decision. Good mentors are firm yet gentle, and insightful beyond belief! What you seek in a mentor is what you want to be. You should be conservative and thorough in assessing why you want to select a particular mentor. You should look at more than just the title of the individual. You really want to think about the values and beliefs of the individual and his or her competencies. You want a good relationship with this person. You want to be able to talk about a laundry list of things such as:

- The culture of the company.
- The political landscape.
- How you are perceived in the organization.
- Negative behaviors you may need to address.
- Work/life balance.

How can you get the most out of your relationship with your mentor?

- Be organized!
- Set an agenda.
- Respect honesty.
- Speak the truth. If you don't understand, say so. If you don't agree, express yourself.
- Learn to LISTEN!
- Don't think that a coach or mentor has all the answers.
- Receive the information provided, knowing that he or she has your best interest at heart.
- Expect good things to come out of the relationship.

According to Catalyst, a nonprofit research organization, "mentoring relationships are particularly important to women and minorities." In a book co-authored by Sheila Wellington and Catalyst, mentoring was listed as "the single most important reason why men tend to rise higher than women." This is not surprising, but it is very telling. Mentors are there to give you insight and to connect you with people you need to know.

> [The new face of today's workforce is putting a huge crack in the armor of the good ol' boy network.]

The good ol' boy network has always served men very well. The new face of today's workforce is putting a huge crack in the armor of the good ol' boy network. I'm not trying to put men down by including this information. The fact of the matter is that our society is undergoing a tremendous transformation. Years ago, it was only the men who got the jobs, so of course they helped each other, and hence the birth of the good ol' boy network. The new face of corporate America has a little of everything. The diverse workforce needs a new infrastructure of support and it's not the good ol' boy club. I can't say it any more directly than that. I know that there is resistance to eliminate the good ol' boy club on the part of those who belong to it. I understand that this has been a source of comfort. It will take courage to make this change. I just hope that the good ol' boys will come to a point where they want to make the change because it is the right thing to do, not because they are afraid they will lose their jobs.

### Serving as a Mentor

Equally important to obtaining a mentor is serving as a mentor. I believe that each of us has a responsibility to give back. It is a wonderful way to add value to others and also to enrich yourself. As we build stronger female leaders, more of them will be ready to mentor younger, developing men and women. You know from seeking a mentor how important the role can be. As a mentor to someone else, you've got to get mentally ready to help guide and develop that person. One word of caution: If a junior person asks you about being a mentor to him or her, make sure that his or her manager is aware of the relationship. Unfortunately, there are still individuals who will get their feathers ruffled if they think someone who reports to them is receiving something that they are not getting. And sometimes managers are concerned that if a person who reports to them receives mentoring from another, it is a sign they aren't providing what is needed. Sounds ridiculous, right? But it happens.

Here are some pointers to help you be the best mentor possible.

- Ask a lot of questions.
- Make sure that the two of you agree on the areas that need to be addressed during your time together.
- Honor the time commitment.
- Openly share your knowledge (successes and failures).
- Don't act as if you have all the answers!
- Be ready to give "tough love."
- Follow up.
- Be sensitive to the culture of the company.
- Give advice, but leave the decision for implementation up to the person being mentored.
- Hold the person being mentored responsible and accountable for assignments that you provide for his or her development.

## Is It Time for a Coach?

If you are looking for a way to advance your career, coaching may be the answer. Coaching is a proven, effective method that positively impacts performance. Coaching can occur in one-on-one and group settings. Coaching in the business environment is relatively new. In the last five years, many corporations have chosen to support their staff by using an outside coach. Every indication is that coaching is not a trend but a recognized, value-added business strategy. In fact, prominent authors, professors, and leadership experts suggest that coaching is a powerful method to help employees achieve greater success.

Coaching is considered to be a critical component in developing leadership skills. Research indicates that coaching contributes to increased productivity and employee satisfaction; it also provides increased financial contributions through innovations and efficiencies. A recent study conducted by MetrixGlobal LLC determined that the benefits and return on investment for a coaching program can be as high as 529 percent. Hiring a coach should be included in your development plan. Many companies will cover the cost if you ask them to. Make sure that you identify the reasons for the coaching and the expected benefits of the program to the company. You'll need to be careful to connect it to productivity, performance improvement, and profitability.

> [ Coaches act as psychologist, friend, mentor, consultant, and accountability partner. ]

The decision to use a business coach requires a lot of thought. I used a coach when I was in corporate. I knew that it was time for a coach because I found myself complaining, always tired, and not as productive as I wanted to be. I was leaving on Sundays and returning on Thursdays. I was totally out of balance. I needed someone who could help me rework my plan. By accident I found a coach who lived in my neighborhood. He was just getting started with his business. I was his pilot case. Even though he was new at the game, the relationship was extremely beneficial. He challenged me to walk my own talk: take responsibility for every part of my life. As I look back on that experience, I am amazed at how effective the right questions can be.

Coaches act as psychologist, friend, mentor, consultant, and accountability partner. They can play a very valuable role in your development plan.

## The World of Coaching

Coaching provides a risk-free, rich environment for learning and development. Areas that are emphasized in coaching include personal effectiveness, leadership development, business acumen, and career development. These broad areas cover an extensive range of competencies and skills. I strongly encourage you to think about an outside coach or mentor. The reason is this: *Often the political pressures that exist internally in the corporate environment prohibit totally honest feedback.*

Some of the potential results of using a coach:

- Increased productivity
- Increased knowledge
- Cross-training opportunities
- Consistent, candid, honest feedback
- Effective working relationships
- Strategic-planning skill development
- Collaborative planning
- Change agent leadership

- Leadership through service
- Self-marketing
- Creating powerful connections
- Effective communication
- Trust, integrity, values
- Interpersonal skills
- Standards and boundaries
- Self-motivation
- Personal business principles
- Networking for success
- Developing a "Personal Value Proposition"
- Conflict resolution
- Thinking and operating strategically

The positive personal improvement and changes are of enormous benefit to any organization. These benefits are realized in the following areas:

- More effective leaders
- Greater individual and team performance
- Enhanced internal/external cross-functional business relationships, leading to better collaborative planning and strategy execution
- Improved communication effectiveness
- Enhanced efficiencies gained through best practice sharing that translate into financial benefits
- Improved productivity leading to enhanced profitability

Recent studies have demonstrated that employee retention is higher when coaching for improved business performance is utilized. Employee retention plays a critical role in an organization's effectiveness. This is yet another benefit that organizations receive as a result of using an outside coach.

[ Recent studies have demonstrated that employee retention is higher when coaching for improved business performance is utilized. ]

Prior to the beginning of the coaching relationship, there is a research period. During this period, there is candid conversation with the coaching participant's manager to gain an understanding about the culture, business challenges, and objectives. In addition, clarity and understanding of other training programs are shared in order to maximize the coaching relationship. There has been significant research that confirms the benefits of training programs. The combination of training programs reinforced by coaching has proven to be extremely impactful. In fact, according to a survey conducted by *Public Personnel Management Magazine,* employees who participated in training programs had a 22 percent increase in productivity. When training was combined with coaching, that figure jumped to 88 percent!

The entire coaching process is focused on obtaining results. Given that coaching is a partnership, goals are established and agreed upon and specific outcomes are identified that facilitate measurement of progress. The goal is to put the learning into action. In order for this to happen, the coach has to create an environment where a participant can share concerns, issues, and opportunities candidly. It is for this reason that coaching sessions are kept confidential. The only exception to this parameter would be if the coach perceived the employee to be in emotional or physical distress.

Here are some tips on developing a mentor/coach relationship and maximizing the benefits from the relationship:

1. Identify the qualities and characteristics of someone you value.
2. Remember that this is a two-way relationship.
3. Don't expect a "bond" overnight. A mentor/coach relationship is just that—a relationship—and relationships take time to develop.
4. Consider mentoring a new employee. You'll find that serving in this capacity will strengthen your knowledge and help you to hone your skills.

## You, Too, Can Be a Coach!

In today's competitive marketplace, finding new ways to increase individual and team performance is not an option—it's a necessity. Leaders have to be able to coach their people to higher levels of performance. As you develop and take on more responsibility within the organization, you will need to develop your coaching skills. Harnessing the greatness of others is not about telling people what to do; it is very much about coaching them and giving them the resources to be successful.

> Harnessing the greatness of others is not about telling a person what to do; it is very much about coaching them and giving them the resources to be successful.

In a recent discussion, a manager relayed to me that "coaching" in the company culture where he is employed is interpreted as a negative. When I asked why, he said that it was because most people who were receiving coaching were being coached out of the company. "Why would a company invest time and money to coach someone out of the company?" I wondered. Being careful not to insult this gentleman whom I had just met, I asked if these people were being coached because they have drug or alcohol problems. Much to my surprise, his answer was no. He went on to say that these were employees who just didn't seem to be able to maintain consistent performance.

The cost of replacing an employee is extremely high from various perspectives, including the learning curve, productivity losses, and recruiting costs. Sometimes managers look at getting rid of an employee as an "easy fix" to a problem. The reality is that there will always be performance issues. For that reason as well as many others, managers must develop their own coaching skills. The mind-set of the manager or leader must also be taken into consideration. In order for coaching to work, the leader must believe in the possibility of developing ordinary people into extraordinary performers.

> Analysts predict that in the next five years there will be a skilled worker shortage.

Managers and leaders must foster an environment where each employee is motivated based upon his or her individual career objectives. Thinking that every employee will respond the same way to a cookie-cutter management style is a mistake. The result is high turnover. This can be avoided by a leader who coaches his or her people on a consistent basis. It is in a company's best interest to retain good talent. A leader must not fall into the trap of believing that every employee will respond in the same way to a particular management style. There are enormous benefits to anyone who receives internal or external coaching. What I'm talking about is adopting a "coaching philosophy" that embraces the notion that we are all responsible for improving each other's performance, day in and day out. The way that leaders are developed at every level of the organization, the way that performance is enhanced with the greatest impact, is to coach with a theory of developing talent, not releasing it.

Analysts predict that in the next five years there will be a skilled worker shortage. With that knowledge, we would all be wise to get the biggest return on the investment we make in developing our people, so they can stay and add the greatest value. How can this be achieved? As a leader within the organization, you will be expected to produce results. To do so you must develop your team. This is where your coaching abilities really come into play. Long gone are the days when the person in charge could demand that people do things without question. To get the maximum performance from your team, you will need to inform, educate, and motivate. Coaching is a great support for all three. As the coach/leader you set the direction, but you also draw out the best in each member to ensure that you achieve the team's goals. I have outlined a list of critical steps that will assist you in this process.

1. **Establish clarity for the organization's goals, vision, and mission.** Employee performance is enhanced when the goals of the organization are clearly understood. Not only should they be understood, but they must be believable and achievable. If the company's vision is to become the number one company in the industry, but market share continues to fall and there

are no signs of innovation that will help to stop the bleeding, then you can expect adequate performance from your people at best. Why would people want to give their all to a ship that is going down? An effective leader is able to stand with confidence and chart a clear course. Then and only then will people be willing to follow.

2. Align each team member's individual position and performance with the company's bottom line.

Sometimes the most powerful way to coach a person is to make her understand that she is valued. What better way is there to make an employee feel valued than to connect what her performance means to the business? Every team member has value, but if your employees don't understand their connection, they may not demonstrate peak performance.

3. Motivation is an individual thing, not one-size-fits-all.

An effective leader must take the time to find out what motivates each and every employee. Being able to provide the right motivators can help you coach your employees to achieve greater performance. A twenty-year seasoned veteran is motivated by compensation and leaving a legacy, not by the carrot of the corner office. However, a recent MBA graduate who has invested eight years in education is extremely motivated by climbing the ladder to obtain the corner office. Find out what's important and valued by each of your employees and then customize a performance motivation program.

4. Set clear performance objectives based upon S.M.A.R.T. (Smart, Measurable, Achievable, Results-Oriented, and Timely) goal setting (refer back to chapter 4).

Most people get the Smart, Measurable, and Timely, but few get the Achievable part. Stretch goals are one thing; unreachable goals are a setup for failure. At the speed that things change today, employees expect that their objectives will change, but the leader should be able to coach the employees on how to get the current objectives accomplished. An effective coach will make sure that plans and objectives are clear and resources are available to make them happen.

5. Stay involved and formulate midpoint correction dates.

Coaching should be both formal and informal. However, a wise coach proactively establishes times to check performance so that corrections can be made. It's important to let people know that you appreciate their hard work. Checkpoints are a great opportunity to do just that. I encourage you, however, to consider giving words of praise anytime you see something worthy of praising. It will go a long way toward building a good relationship between you and your employees. Then, when the tough love has to be shared, it will help to balance things out. This creates a win-win!

6. Ask for feedback on your communication style, clarity of direction, and support.

An effective coach realizes that even the best of the best have blind spots. You can't realize the full impact of your coaching unless you are willing to listen. Take the time needed to solicit direct and indirect feedback. I am definitely partial to face-to-face discussions; I believe you should be able to say anything to a person's face that you would say behind his or her back. And a leader should be transparent. If everyone is pursuing the same goal, then ego shouldn't get in the way of healthy, fruitful discussions.

### 7. Know when to have tough conversations.

There are times when tough conversations are needed to help to get an employee back on track. Even when you have to engage in a tough discussion, it can be done within a spirit of honesty, caring, and trust. The best coaches know the value of setting the tone of the conversation so that the words that are shared can be received. If the people on your team honestly believe that you are trying to help them develop, then giving tough feedback will be easy. Open and honest communication, on an ongoing basis, is the best way to ensure that people are not blindsided by an assessment of poor performance.

Apply these tips and others you learn during time spent with your own coach or mentor. Remember to keep the elements that resonate with who you are, and leave the rest behind.

## Points Worth Remembering

- Identify and tap into every available resource.
- What you seek in a mentor is what you want to be. Consider his or her values, beliefs, and competencies.
- Coaching contributes to increased productivity and employee satisfaction.
- Developing coaching skills will provide critical support to your role as a leader in developing the greatness of others.

# Hold On, Change Is Coming

*"The only thing we know about the future is that it is going to be different."*
—Peter Drucker

## Change Is a Way of Life

The one thing that is constant today is change. Change is not a bad thing. It can actually be a very good thing if you are willing to look at it as an opportunity. I recently read a quote that really caused me to think: "Change doesn't guarantee success, but success cannot occur without change." So often we fear change, but you won't be successful without truly embracing change as an opportunity. Even the most evil occurrences that have taken place in this world have yielded positive outcomes. Take the September 11, 2001 terrorist tragedy as an example. It certainly changed America, and perhaps the world, forever! Despite the thousands of lost lives, that occurrence for many people was a positive catalyst for rethinking their priorities—including their professional lives. It was as if people suddenly realized that life is short and they want to make sure that they are spending whatever time they have wisely.

> [ "Change doesn't guarantee success, but success cannot occur without change." ]

The vast scope of changes will continue to spill over into the workplace. Most people will work for as many as ten companies in their work lives. I don't necessarily believe that these constant employment shifts will be beneficial to the productivity of corporations as a whole. In an article by Elayne Robertson Demby entitled "Loyalty May Become Cool Again," she suggests that as baby boomers near retirement and company knowledge becomes more important than ever, long-term employees will become valuable once again. The notion of employees becoming free agents is growing and will only change if leaders in organizations take actions such as those recommended in this book.

In Demby's article, reference is made to a comment offered by Deborrah Himsel of Avon. She shares her belief that both employees and employers are looking more at building long-term relationships. Companies are now seeing that committed employees lead to increased productivity.

An opportunity exists for those who want to advance to capitalize on the continuous changes that are occurring. I believe that individuals who rise to this challenge will advance more quickly and have greater impact than they could have ever imagined. It calls for a total commitment to empowerment!

## Calculated Risks

Change requires that you be willing to take a risk. One of my very first big promotions was to the position of district manager. I was so happy about the promotion that I forgot to ask what geography the district covered. I found out the district was in South Central Los Angeles and that I would be the first woman in the company ever to lead a district that was in an inner city. These districts had always been reserved for men. Working in an inner city had not been part of my plan, but I knew I had to successfully handle this role and several others in order to get to the position that I wanted—vice president. If I hadn't been flexible, I would have missed out on a big opportunity. As it turns out, it was a blessing in disguise. After overcoming a lot of hurdles, I was able to accomplish things that had never been done in the industry, let alone in the company. The message is this: *Don't be afraid to take the bend in the road just because you can't see what's coming up.*

The key to embracing change is to have a flexible mindset. You have to look for new opportunities on a daily basis. In today's environment, change is constant. If you're not able to use change to your advantage, you will have a difficult time achieving your goals.

## THE SEVEN LAWS OF CHANGE

1. Change is inevitable!
2. Change dictates that you make a personal choice!
3. Change is an opportunity!
4. Change requires flexibility!
5. Change management requires a plan!
6. Change requires self-leadership!
7. Change builds resiliency!

Change is difficult, whether it is positive or negative. As a leader, you will not only have to manage change for yourself, you will also have to get others to handle it. Most people think they are able to handle change fairly easily. The exact opposite is true. Change requires you to leave your comfort zone, and that's hard. I have found that most people resist change because they don't understand how the change will benefit them. The fear that we associate with change is about letting go of what we know, with what we are familiar. John Kotter, in his new book *The Heart of Change,* emphasizes the importance of getting people to *feel* the change. He calls it the "see-feel-change dynamic." In order to feel, people have to be touched emotionally. "This requires an appeal to the heart," Kotter says. This is a remarkable advance in the study of change management. For years, organizations have struggled with how to get their employees to change. Lots of organizations have been successful in introducing change, but few have been able to make it stick.

## UNDERSTANDING THE CHANGING LANDSCAPE

Part of the formula for success includes gaining and maintaining a keen awareness and understanding of the landscape or the culture of the organization. Your company may not be making the change from old paradigms to new paradigms at the same speed as another company. You may need to be the catalyst to help your company move from an old paradigm approach to a new one.

The chart below outlines some key work environment shifts. Take some time to digest this information and think about where you are mentally as it relates to each topic. Are you stuck in the old paradigms? If so, you need to make significant changes. If you feel as if you are moving toward the new paradigms, then you may need to turn up the burners.

| Old Paradigms | New Paradigms |
|---|---|
| Job Security | Job Protection |
| Company Responsibility | Personal Responsibility |
| Singular Focus | Holistic Focus |
| Company Image | Work/Life Balance |
| Top-Down Management | Self-Management |
| Speak When Spoken To | Initiate Dialogue |
| Minimal Work Change | Constant Change |
| Company-Designed Careers | Self-Designed Careers |
| Dictatorship | Leadership |

## Tapping into Your Tolerance for Change

I would be less than honest if I told you that building a successful career and climbing the ladder is easy. It may be the hardest thing you've ever done! It requires self-leadership. What we've been talking about this far in the book is at the very core of self-leadership. Getting in touch with your values and beliefs will help you live and function in integrity. Setting boundaries will help you continue to focus on pursuing balance. It will take courage to stay true to your beliefs and values as you advance your career. And it will take courage to make changes.

> The new world will be built on principles and beliefs that allow all employees to be optimized regardless of their skin color, background, or gender. And I believe that women will lead the way in creating this new business world!

The business world is undergoing a lot of positive change. But there is much work yet to be done. I believe that you (yes, *YOU* ) can play a role in creating a new world. The new world will be built on principles and beliefs that allow all employees to be optimized regardless of their skin color, background, or gender. And I believe that women will lead the way in creating this new business world! Why do I say this? Because we know how it feels to be rejected just because we don't have hair on our chests. We know that there is no one-size-fits-all, cookie-cutter approach to connecting life to work and work to life. In order for women to accelerate in business, we have got to be willing to take risks. Those of you who will experience breakthrough success will do so by reinventing the rules.

[ People should be promoted based upon their ability to get the job done. ]

What does reinventing the rules mean? It means getting to the top and eliminating private networks that exclude certain groups because of race or gender. It also means that each of you has the opportunity to change the subjectivity that is currently associated with who gets promoted and why. How many of you report to an individual who doesn't have the skill set needed to be in the role? Does it make you mad? Do you resent having to train this person, knowing that you are totally capable of handling the job? Do you think this person was only promoted because he or she was connected to the right person at the top? Do you feel in your spirit that an injustice has occurred? If you understand the disappointment that these kinds of experiences can cause, then you'll understand why the rules need to be reinvented.

People should be promoted based upon their ability to get the job done, not because they are connected. In order for this to become reality we have to have senior executives who are willing to adopt transparent succession planning. Career goal setting cannot be performed without a very clear understanding of the succession planning process within the organization. This is assuming that you want to stay with the company. If you are at a point where you are open to looking outside, then that's another story. I emphasize this point because I don't want you to go through this exercise and be disappointed because your goals can't be achieved within your current organization.

Your career success is directly tied to the opportunities for you to develop and flourish. It is critical, therefore, that you set career goals with a clear picture of the environment that needs to be in place in order for your goals to become a reality.

Not too long ago, if you had told a company that there would be a female CEO at the helm, or if you told them that employees would demand flexible work schedules, you would have been laughed out of the building. It took the conviction and courage of individuals just like you and me to lead the way for these situations to become reality. I believe that each of us has the wisdom inside to meet challenges with success, provided we believe in the cause. Knowledge is power! Self-knowledge is critical in order for your career goals to be meaningful.

Leaders must have the vision in order to persuade others to follow. The reality is that there are few examples of companies that have truly been able to create an environment rich in opportunities for people of different genders and backgrounds. Most of the people who are in charge of corporations today are male, white, and from an era where women, minorities, and others are sometimes seen but definitely not heard. Perhaps this statement sounds a bit extreme. The fact is, almost 90 percent of all companies are run by men, and most of those are white men. A lot of these men have stay-at-home wives who play golf or tennis at the country club several times a week. So when you approach them about work/life balance, they can't process what you are saying because they have no experience in it. When you offer up the idea that diversity, recruitment, and retention should be tied to performance and compensation, they are immediately placed on the defensive. It will take courage to face the critics and naysayers.

I strongly encourage you to spend the time needed to gain an honest appreciation of how you tolerate change. It is only with this understanding that you will be able to make a difference that is significant and lasting. I do not know of any leaders who have climbed the ladder without adding or contributing some new concept, new best practice, or new business practice. The key word is new. Interjecting newness means change, and change translates into moving people out of their comfort zones.

As a leader, you will probably have to demonstrate by example your commitment to change. Let's first find out whether you embrace change. Here's an exercise that you might find useful. I have used this exercise in my workshops and it has always proven to be enlightening and somewhat surprising.

Rate yourself on a scale of 1 to 6 (1 being the lowest, and 6 being the highest).

- I am willing to embrace change.
  1——2——3——4——5——6

- Change causes my confidence level to fluctuate.
  1——2——3——4——5——6

- I am comfortable leading change.
  1——2——3——4——5——6

- I know how to transfer passion for change to other people.
  1——2——3——4——5——6

- I recognize that change is difficult for people, so I am careful to flex my behavior in order to meet people where they are instead of where I am in the change process.
  1——2——3——4——5——6

- I know what processes to put in place in order to infuse behavioral changes that last.
  1——2——3——4——5——6

- I believe it is important to get the buy-in of the entire team to facilitate a change movement.
  1——2——3——4——5——6

I am not going to ask you what your total score came to, because it doesn't matter. So why did I ask you to go through it? I asked you to do it because it builds *your* awareness. You don't know what you don't know! What matters is your awareness of how, as a leader, you can impact change for yourself and for others. Change shouldn't just be something that is talked about. It should be visible. Let me give you an example.

> Change shouldn't just be something that is talked about. It should be visible.

In my corporate experience, I worked under the leadership of three different company presidents. When the last president came aboard, we all knew that drastic change was about to happen. And to be honest, for the most part I was excited about this change. The new president came into the company with a strong desire to make a statement that there would be more than talk about change. The first element of change was the introduction that the company would be customer-focused. There are lots of ways that this message could be reinforced. It could be reinforced through standard operating procedures. It could be reinforced through quarterly business addresses. But the more impactful way was to do something that people could see on a daily basis. The president recognized that for the employees to truly believe in this change, there would need to be some visible demonstration. The visible example was the removal of the pictures of past presidents of the company from the walls of the home office. Those pictures were replaced with pictures of the company's top customers. That visible change sent the message clearly: *This company will put its customers first!*

Change can come in so many ways. As organizations grapple with what I believe are the top three areas of focus—growth, people, and profitability—proactive change will be the prescription of order. Change is a way of life. Only those individuals and companies that stay abreast of these changes and proactively address the opportunities that these changes bring will experience success. What, then, are the key issues or opportunities for companies that want to succeed in the twenty-first century?

1. ADOPTING A FULLY INTEGRATED BUSINESS MODEL. Obtaining synergies will enable a company to gain efficiencies. Growth in a stagnant market will occur only for those companies that meet the changing needs of a savvy consumer. The ability to proactively meet the requirements of the global consumer will lead to increased profitability. Limited resources will continue to be an issue, so it will be imperative that all departments are focused on activities that complement each other's work and add value to the achievement of the company goals. Reducing and eliminating redundant work will contribute positively to the bottom line, which will always remain the top priority for any company that lives to satisfy the stockholder.
   a. There is so much information available it's almost to the point of overload. Not only will companies have to keep up with technology, they will also have to be able to use technology to enhance the company's ability to communicate more effectively with its consumer base. Progressive organizations will challenge themselves and technology manufacturers to help achieve integration throughout the organization.
   b. To achieve a cross-functional team business approach, it will take a willingness to break down the silos. This means that IT, marketing, sales, business development, finance, production, and human resources will all have to be marching to the same drum, pursuing the same goals. This is not an easy

challenge. It can, however, be overcome with support of process and data exchange.

c. New marketing techniques and new ways to speak to the consumer at the point of sale will be the key to maintaining and gaining market share. Customized market plans by region will become the norm, given the changing demographics within the country. As an example, Hispanics and Asians are the two fastest-growing demographic populations in the United States. What do these developments mean in terms of marketing and sales? Another example would be the "woman" factor. A woman influences 80 percent of all purchases. How can a company ensure that it is properly positioned to capitalize on this huge reality? It will take the talent, energy, and effort of the entire organization to maximize these changes. It will also take solidifying business relationships, which leads us to the next critical issue.

d. Business relationships between manufacturers and retailers will be developed based on fact-based selling. Retailers will expect customized promotional offers. In order to achieve superior execution and effectively manage inventory, organizations will be forced to rethink the entire supply chain. This is one of the few remaining areas where synergies can translate into bottom-line profit contributions.

> [ Successful organization will embrace diversity in its broadest context. ]

2. DEVELOPING DIVERSE LEADERSHIP. Diversity is not restricted to color or gender—it goes so far beyond that. Diversity

includes innovation, looking at the business from a different perspective, and developing new models and approaches. Successful organizations will embrace diversity in its broadest context.

a. The consumer base is extremely diverse; therefore, organizations must develop a diverse workforce in order to market effectively. In the twenty-first century, diverse leadership has been noted as one of the most significant success factors by *Fortune* magazine. Diverse leadership includes all cultures and all backgrounds, but there is a clear skew toward women and minorities. In order to attract the best talent, organizations will have to establish themselves as an "employer of choice," which means being extremely flexible, culturally sensitive, and acknowledging that the good ol' boy network is no longer effective. Successful organizations will adopt policies and philosophies that support diversity and build diverse leadership as a key strategic business activity.
b. Buyers are becoming more diverse. The days of margin being used as leverage are gone. We can thank Wal-Mart for that market dynamic. The opportunity to adopt a more knowledgeable consulting relationship with your most strategic customers will be a top priority. Shifting from a "gut" sales approach to an "analytical, data-driven" sales approach will separate the winners from the losers.
c. Global economics will drive the need to reexamine every aspect of business. Those organizations that have diverse talents will be able to get into new markets more quickly and experience profitability sooner.

3. RECRUITING AND RETENTION. There is an overwhelming amount of evidence that supports the belief that there will be a skilled labor shortage in the next ten years. According to information posted by the U.S. Labor Department, the unemployment rate in seven years could be at 2 percent, meaning that many companies are going to have to acquire qualified workers from other sources. Traditional recruiting includes headhunters, newspapers, and conventions. In the twenty-first century, recruiting will begin at grade schools, with companies sponsoring programs that can formulate relationships earlier in the lives of potential employees and potential customers. Employers will look to their current employees to find new employees, either through the community or through alumni relationships. Couple that forecast with the uncertainty of how long baby boomers will remain in the workforce, and organizations will have to address their cultures in order to meet the expectations of four generations. To get the talent needed to maintain a competitive edge, companies will have to begin to think of recruiting in nontraditional locations. Proactive companies are already investing in developing high school and college programs that build awareness of their companies. Whether it's providing computers, mentors, or leadership development, companies are heavily engaging in outreach programs that will position them as "employers of choice" for the future.

These top issues clearly support the belief that "people development" will be one of the most critical success factors in the twenty-first century. Technology is available just about everywhere in the world. Skilled workers who can properly utilize technology to support execution of the strategy are not available everywhere. Only the employers who have the "right" vision, the "right" culture, and the "right" business model will be standing at the end of the twenty-first century.

## The Colors of the WorkForce Rainbow

One of my clients asked me to help him understand what changes would need to be made to his organization's culture for it to be viewed as a "good place to work." Knowing what I thought I understood to be the culture, my response was, "You've got to create affinity groups. You've got to bring life to the work/life balance policy. You've got to embrace women leaders. You've got to . . . "

"Stop!" he said. "That sounds like a very long process."

"The process itself isn't long," I responded, "but changing people's minds and hearts will take a while. If you are serious about being considered as a top employer, then you and your leadership will have to understand that the workforce is changing, and respond to that change."

> [ The twenty-first-century workforce is dramatically different. ]

The twenty-first-century workforce is dramatically different. The changes go far beyond gender and color of skin. They extend into the way work is viewed. This includes the way work is conducted. It also includes the relationships that exist at work and the emotions that are expressed at work. We know that the business environment is extremely dynamic. We know that the consumer is changing.

We know that the market becomes more global every day. We know that the workforce is changing. We know that companies that develop diverse talent gain a competitive advantage in pursuing their end customers. We know that there is richness in diversity. What don't we know? We don't know why some companies see the writing on the wall and why others still think of diversity as a black/white or male/female issue.

The facts cannot be refuted. By the year 2020, more than half of the population entering the workforce will be Hispanics, African-Americans, Asians, or other non-Caucasian cultures, as reported by *Workforce Management Magazine*. According to the U.S. Department of Labor, by 2050 the U.S. population is expected to increase by 50 percent, and minority groups will make up nearly half the population. Hispanics are the fastest-growing segment of the population. Approximately 61 million Americans will retire over the next three years. Where is the talent to replace these workers? Employment Policy Foundation President Ed Potter says that within the next five years the demand for labor will begin to exceed supply. Without changes to policies that guide the workplace and its employees, the nation will be unable to maintain its historic rate of economic growth. Companies and leaders have got to wrap their minds around what these trends mean in terms of the business model and culture.

African-Americans, Asians, and Hispanics were estimated to be 25 percent of the U.S. consumer base at the end of 2000. The combined spending power of Hispanics and African-Americans is nearing $650 million. So why is there such a struggle to embrace diversity as a critical component of the business strategy? Well, it boils down to this: *People don't like to change, even when it is good.* The pain points for some organizations haven't been intense enough to cause them to develop an appetite for this kind of change. If you are reading this book and your company has not moved in this direction, don't worry; the pain will soon be great enough to stimulate change!

Even if the "old school" thinkers can't make the change because it's the right thing to do, perhaps their daughters will be a source of motivation and inspiration. I had the following revelation in one of my executive coaching sessions. I was coaching a vice president of a large consumer goods organization. He truly is a good guy. He just didn't understand what diversity really meant. And he was paralyzed by fear. His fear was that he would be put out to pasture and left for dead. We had many conversations about the changing workforce. He truly wanted to change his viewpoints and improve his appreciation for diversity. He also knew that it was in his best interest to make this paradigm shift. But he just didn't know how.

> He wanted his daughters to be valued for who they are and what they bring to the table.

It wasn't until he shared the work we were doing with his family that he experienced the "aha" moment. He told me that one evening at dinner, the entire family (his wife and two daughters) was talking about the girls' future. His daughters are smart and ambitious. Each of them shared her desire to become a senior executive. It suddenly hit him that his daughters would have to face and overcome good ol' boy thinking. It scared him into reality. He realized he did not want his daughters to have the same experiences that the women and minorities he worked with were having. He wanted his daughters to be valued for who they are and what they bring to the table. This "aha" moment stirred a deep emotion in him. As a result, he got involved in supporting affinity groups. He became a champion to help his colleagues and the organization understand the importance of creating a culture where everyone can thrive, not just survive. It was truly a beautiful moment for me personally. I knew that I touched someone else to the point of positive change. Where is that VP now? He's still using the information that I armed him with, plus his personal experience, to lead the charge. What information did I provide him? I'll give it to you too!

1. The demographics shift data outlined in the paragraphs above.
2. An understanding that it wasn't his way or their way. It would be a new way that he would play a critical role in shaping.
3. Workforce trends painting a clear picture that white males would no longer be the majority of the workforce.
4. Case studies of leaders who were embracing diversity as a key component of the business strategy.

I clearly remember once sitting in my boss's office having a rather intense discussion about diversity. At that point in my career I was at the vice president level. I had a self-imposed sense of responsibility to help the organization develop diverse leaders at every level. We were discussing why it was good for the organization to promote more women and minorities. He jokingly said, "We have you, isn't that enough?" But it wasn't a joke. It was coming out of his very soul. I must have looked shocked at his statement because he asked if I understood that it was a joke. This is the kind of leadership that needs to be removed from any position of influence. It is this old-school thinking that is keeping companies from experiencing higher levels of success through building diverse leadership.

[ It is this old-school thinking that is keeping companies from experiencing higher levels of success through building diverse leadership. ]

I had seen my boss react this way before. When I introduced the idea of developing a Women's Leadership Forum, he immediately resisted. Until, of course, he heard that the president of the company was endorsing the group. He couldn't understand what we were going to do. He asked me if we were going to take our bras off and picket at the front of the building. Can you imagine? This conversation about the Women's Leadership Forum happened in 1998. He couldn't understand how it would be beneficial to the women of the organization and to the organization at large. He had no clue as to the frustration levels being experienced by women and minorities within the organization. The sad reality is that I don't think he cared. What was most disappointing to me about this experience is that my boss and I were not that far apart in age or experience.

## Nontraditional Benefits

Job sharing and flextime are expected benefits in the eyes of today's workforce. And this expectation is not restricted to women. The traditional family unit has been redefined.

There are a growing number of single fathers. And even married parents need flexibility. Adults are waiting later in life to have children, so when they have children they want time to be with their newborns. A friend of mine, John B., is thirty-eight and an upper-mid-level manager with a major consumer goods organization. In the year 2000 he and his wife had their first baby. They were both so excited. They videotaped her progression over the nine months leading up to the baby's birth. They researched names. They sang to the baby in the womb. They were really into it. After the birth, John B. realized that he really wanted to have some time with his new baby. A few days wouldn't do; he wanted at least six weeks off.

John B. has been an employee of his company for a number of years. He has been promoted several times and is in line for a vice president position. None of this stopped him from going to his boss and asking for six weeks off with pay. He shared with me his plan to go in and ask for paternity leave. The company had no policy for fathers to take leave for the birth of a baby. This time off wouldn't be covered under any other plan. He knew that he could take vacation, but he didn't want to. He wanted to be given the same benefits as a female parent. He built his case, presented it, and took six weeks off with pay. As a result of his leadership, the company adopted a new paternity leave policy. He wanted the company to understand and embrace his need for this time. Right on! Right on!

There are some companies that like being at the cutting edge of new developments. Ford Motor Company is one of those. Ford has just recently taken its day care and split it in half. Half the day care is reserved for child care and the remainder is reserved for elder care. Ford has come to terms with the fact that America has an aging population. Baby boomers comprise the largest portion of that company's employee base. As a result, elder care has risen to obtain importance equal to child care.

Elder care is definitely a trend that will cause organizations to change. Baby boomers will be faced with the reality of elder care for their parents. The May 2000 issue of *HR* magazine featured an article entitled "The Elder Care Gap: The Need for Elder Care Continues to Grow. Are Employers Meeting the Demand?" The article focuses on Fannie Mae in Washington, D.C. Fannie Mae's has every reason to implement a formal elder care benefits policy. Of its 3,900 employees, 70 percent are expected to take on elder care responsibilities within the next several years. Fannie Mae appointed an on-site manager to provide free consultations. The net impact of Fannie Mae's decision to proactively address this opportunity translated into worker productivity. In fact, for every dollar that Fannie Mae spends on elder care benefits, the company forecasts a $1.50 return in the form of higher productivity, retention, and reduced absenteeism and turnover. Fannie Mae was definitely on the cutting edge. If you want to be able to position yourself as a top employer, you will have to be prepared to address this trend.

Telecommuting and job sharing (where two people share one position) were also found to have a positive impact on productivity. In fact, a survey by True Careers in Reston, Virginia, found that 92 percent of employees think the ability to telework would be a key factor in their decision to accept a job. In another study conducted by Positively Broadband Campaign, of the participants interviewed, approximately one-third said they would prefer the option to telework over higher pay.

A recent study conducted by Hewitt Associates discovered that the percentage of companies offering work/life benefits increased in 2000 despite the economic downturn that occurred in the latter part of the year.

- 91 percent of companies offer some kind of child care assistance to their employees.
- 49 percent of all companies offer some form of elder care.
- Flexible scheduling arrangements are offered by 73 percent of businesses.
- Flextime was offered by 58 percent of companies.
- Part-time employment options were offered by 48 percent.
- Work-at-home options were offered by 29 percent.
- Job sharing was an option at 28 percent of companies.
- Compressed work weeks were available at 21 percent of companies.

How does the organization you are currently employed with stack up against this information?

Each year, the Society for Human Resources Management surveys U.S. businesses to find out who's offering what benefits and why. In 1999 there was a significant increase in flexible work schedules. That trend continues today, and all indications are based upon the fact that the changing demographics of the workforce will continue. These are the types of issues and opportunities that a senior leader must think about and proactively manage. We have to accept that loyalty is a thing of the past and make the needed adjustments in order to retain good people. The changes that you will face in your development will center around three critical areas: culture, career development, and people connections. If you find a way to positively impact these areas, your organization will be able to recruit and retain top talent, and it will be positioned to add tremendous value that will translate into profit.

## Beyond the Glass Ceiling

One of my male employees initially told me that it would be difficult to work for me because he had never worked for a woman before. This was not the first time I had heard this. You can imagine how surprised I was when he later walked into my office and said, "I've never been happier with a boss." I had to know why. What he shared with me is actually one of the reasons why I wanted to write a book. He said that women are more emotional and more caring than men. He had never worked as hard and had as much fun! He said that he went the extra mile because he truly believed that I cared. I'm not sharing this with you to pat myself on the back or to say that female leaders are better than male leaders. I share it with you to illustrate that the twenty-first-century workforce wants to be connected. They want a reason to be productive. They want to know that their managers care. A recent *Fast Company* article said that the reason cited by 80 percent of the people for leaving organizations is the lack of a relationship with their manager. People don't leave companies—they leave managers.

> [ . . . the twenty-first-century workforce wants to be connected. They want a reason to be productive. ]

The next generation of employees wants more than truth; they also seek an emotional connection inside and outside. Marcus Buckingham, author of *First Break All the Rules,* puts it this way: "The challenge . . . for the future is for companies to figure out a way to extend relationships beyond price and engage their customers on an emotional level." There is no denying that the landscape is changing. The diverse workforce wants to be both valued and developed. As more and more women climb the corporate ladder, they are prepared to take whatever steps necessary to fulfill their professional objectives, including walking out the door.

[ People don't leave companies— they leave managers. ]

A recent Korn Ferry survey of 425 women executives found that the main reason for leaving their old jobs was that they wanted a larger role in running a company. There is a growing and disturbing trend of women leaving big corporations to be more intimately involved in smaller companies. If this trend continues, valuable talent will be lost; more importantly, valued resources to transform outdated leadership behaviors will be lost. "Professional growth, power, and money were the big drivers in influencing women to leave corporate jobs in the past five years—not the glass ceiling, balance, or personal life. Companies cannot afford to lose a generation of women leaders. In today's world, talent is the primary source of competitive advantage," says Caroline Nahas of *Fast Company*.

[ There is a growing and disturbing trend of women leaving big corporations to be more intimately involved in smaller companies. ]

Corporate America will have to make major adjustments in order to embrace women as leaders. As of January 2003, only two women, Carla Fiornia (Hewlett-Packard) and Andrea Jung (Avon), were CEOs in Fortune 500 companies. Women are extremely close to making up half the work-force, but their climb up the corporate ladder continues to be slowed by an uneven playing field. Women want to experience job satisfaction. I sense that this strong desire will drive them to attempt to transform their current organizations' work environments. But if the corporation doesn't respond, they are prepared to exercise their choices. I love the way former mayor Rudy Giuliani in his book *Leadership* talks about the responsibility of leaders to develop appropriate structures. He asserts that a leader must form a team of people who bring out the best in each other and are willing to take risks.

[ Women want to experience job satisfaction. I sense that this strong desire will drive them to attempt to transform their current organizations' work environments. ]

It is unimaginable that a company would not want to develop the most diverse talent possible, given the diverse population of their consumer base. Tapping the talents of the work-force at large will be a critical success factor. Unfortunately, there is still a perception that women are not as capable in a leadership position as men are. That is total nonsense! The sooner organizations get on board with developing women leaders, the better their chances for sustained success will be.

Kimberly-Clark is a company that has done a good job in the area of developing an environment where women and minorities are encouraged to grow. *Fortune* magazine and Great Places to Work Institute ranked Kimberly-Clark on the updated list of 100 Best Places to Work in America. The president says that Kimberly-Clark has always striven to be among the best, from recruiting, developing, and maintaining employees, to manufacturing and marketing the best products in the world.

I recently had the privilege of being on the platform with Jim Keyes, CEO and president of the world's largest convenience store chain, 7-Eleven. Jim's opening remarks focused on the objectives and challenges that were ahead for 7-Eleven. He said that in order for the company to reach its goals, 7-Eleven would need to develop more women leaders. He referenced the strong strategic desire for 7-Eleven to gain more female shoppers to balance their heavy percentage of male shoppers. He said that in order to attract female shoppers, 7-Eleven would have to stock products that were used most often by the female consumer. Jim acknowledged that his company had not been as successful as it would have liked to have been in recruiting top diverse talents. But he said the organization was committed not only to recruiting but also to developing and retaining diverse talent in order to meet the demands of 7-Eleven's consumer.

I applaud Jim Keyes for his boldness in admitting that 7-Eleven is underdeveloped in this area and for his willingness to step up to the plate to make the necessary changes. How many other organizations need to do just that? The window of opportunity is closing. Better wake up and smell the coffee!

## Points Worth Remembering

- The two critical success factors for leadership in the twenty-first century are embracing change as an opportunity and valuing differences of others.
- If you're not able to use change to your advantage, you will have a difficult time achieving your goals.
- Women can play a critical role in guiding the success of corporate America in the twenty-first century if they are willing to reinvent the rules.
- Nontraditional benefits such as paternity leave, flexible schedules, and in-house facilities for both child care and elder care will become the norm in the twenty-first century.
- Leaders must recognize the changing landscape within their organizations. They must develop the ability to drive needed organizational change in order to respond to the needs of the changing workforce and the changing consumer.

# Facing the Future: Taking Your Rightful Leadership Position

*"Those who are successful see things differently than most people. They create their own reality. Successful people, most of the time, choose to see the positive."*

—Vincent A. Roazzi

## Pillars of Excellence

To experience continued success throughout the twenty-first century, you will have to make a commitment to continuous learning. Long gone are the days when you got a degree and that was enough. The speed of change will continue to be mind-boggling. Technological advances will open a whole new way of life. In order to keep up, you must embrace lifelong learning. The knowledge economy will continue to place a focus on organizations valuing their people as the key critical component to success. As the next generation takes the leadership role in senior management positions, there will be greater emphasis placed on creating a family environment and less emphasis placed on hierarchical power plays. Instead, strong leaders will look to leverage both the intellectual and relational power of their workforce. This will require a different leadership style—one that is far more partnering in foundation and inspirational in scope.

> [ The knowledge economy will continue to place a focus on organizations valuing their people as the key critical component to success. ]

Leaders will still remain responsible for getting results. This will never change. If you are truly interested in reaching the upper echelons of the organization, you will have to bring home the bacon, which in business terms means *get the results*. But how you get it done is what will be different. The higher level of global competition will drive new levels of performance expectations. These expectations will only be fulfilled if the leader focuses on people as the greatest asset of the organization. Great leaders will display strong personal values and seek new ways to demonstrate the value that they have for others.

To get the kind of results that will be expected, you will have to stay on top of the changes and trends that affect your business. And you will have to be able to make predictions about the way those trends will affect the business. At the end of the day, we are all paid to add value that translates into profits for the organization. You need to understand that part of your role as a leader will be to introduce new concepts, despite the fact that the organization might not be ready to accept them. When I was a section sales manager in Los Angeles during the late '90s, there was a significant growth in the Hispanic population. At the time, the company had no ethnic marketing initiative. I asked my team to give me insight on what offers would be appealing to this group. I also connected with the Chamber of Commerce as well as the Mexican American Grocers Association. I built a proposal for a pilot program and submitted it to my manager. His immediate response was that the company wasn't ready for a program of this nature. I must admit I hadn't anticipated a "no" response, and I was extremely disappointed. I could see the opportunity but I couldn't convince the right people. I hadn't painted a picture that was so good, no one was threatened and no one could say no.

Here's the part that I hadn't included and a piece of information that you will want to make a permanent mental note of: *I didn't fully explain what the cost of not doing something would be.* Once I painted the right picture, I got the authorization to move forward with the pilot program. That program resulted in a 25 percent increase in sales. The pilot became a full-blown program and was rolled out nationally to help the company capitalize on Hispanic growth in Florida, New York, and Texas. Paying attention to the trends resulted in my developing a program that got the attention of the president of the company. This exposure was enough to open the door for my next promotion.

Adopt a personal business principle to stay on top of market developments that can represent an opportunity for the company. Scan *The Wall Street Journal* and *Business Week* on a weekly basis. Another of my favorite magazines is *Fast Company.* It's a great business magazine that offers good insight on trends and changes that will impact the way business is conducted. Faith Popcorn, a noted futurist, predicts that by the year 2010, 90 percent of all consumer goods will be home delivered. What would a consumer behavior trend like home delivery mean to your organization? Equally important is the need to maintain a clear understanding of the company's short- and long-term strategies. And you'll need to fully understand how each department fits into the strategies. This is why I am such a believer in the benefit of cross-functional experience. Cross-functional experience is gained from working in multiple departments, so don't be afraid to embrace lateral moves as a part of your career plan. When you adopt a personal best practice of continuous learning, it's very easy to see the benefit of cross-functional experience.

[ . . . no one is indispensable, not even you. ]

There are several other activities you might want to incorporate into your business principles. Think about participating in a share group that hosts monthly meetings where best practices can be shared and issues can be discussed. This will keep you from falling into the tunnel vision trap. It is so easy to bury yourself and just work. Keep your ear to the ground and build your connections with people at multiple levels in multiple industries to keep your value contribution to the organization high.

Another good business principle to keep you humble is this: *Accept that no one is indispensable, not even you.* Don't make the mistake of thinking that the organization can't live without you. It can! You can't get so focused on results that you compromise other important facets of being a leader. I have seen people who were consistently the number one performers, who suddenly had a lapse of judgment, got involved in unethical behavior, and then got fired. There is no tolerance for blunders. I'm not talking about little bitty mistakes. I'm talking about significant poor judgment. Even one slip-up is enough to make people question your credibility. *Always* take the high road. Don't let yourself get sucked into activities that do not align with your values and beliefs. Resist the temptation to adopt bad practices just because doing so is acceptable behavior for some.

Keep your focus on getting results that count and building the kind of diverse team that will keep you performing at the highest level possible. I strongly suggest that you develop your own list of personal business principles. These principles will become your foundation for achieving consistently high results. I have listed some that I use as my guiding principles. I know that you'll find enormous benefits from spending time to develop your own. I suggest this to every client that I coach. Many have told me that by thinking about these principles, writing them down, and taking the time to evaluate their behavior against them, their performance has had a dramatic improvement. Your principles should be solid, not fluid. If you take the time to think this exercise all the way through, you shouldn't have to change your principles; as you grow and develop, however, you may decide to add new ones. Here are a few examples of personal principles that will enhance your leadership effectiveness:

- Integrity is at the root of everything that I do.
- I commit to expressing value for others on a consistent basis.
- I will honor my personal values and beliefs without compromise.
- Excellent performance is the gold standard.

## Valuing People

As a leader, you must be capable of establishing an environment where, based upon trust, employees are empowered to complete their tasks but are also held accountable for results. Diversity of thought will be so highly respected that it will be unnecessary for you as the leader to hand-hold. Virtually self-directed teams will require strong communication skills.

[ The cultures that will develop in the business world will have to become less hierarchical and bureaucratic. ]

The job descriptions for leaders in the new frontier will focus far more on relationship and change management. As a result, strong interpersonal skills will enhance your ability to connect and build the kind of relationships that will foster team development. To effectively manage and lead these teams, the leader will be required to flex his or her style. To motivate the team, greater emphasis will need to be placed on being compassionate and helping others achieve the highest level of productivity by aligning their passions with their jobs.

The cultures that will develop in the business world will have to become less hierarchical and bureaucratic. There will be less emphasis placed on the top person. I believe that the good ol' boy network will be replaced as a result of the demographic shifts in the workforce that I referenced in the previous chapter, but also because there simply won't be a tolerance for that kind of behavior. John Kotter suggests in his book *Leading Change* that organizations will become far more transparent and inclusive.

Warren Bennis makes the observation that the rapidly changing environment will present new challenges for leaders. He suggests that individual heroes will be replaced with collaborative teams and partnerships. I believe this translates into leaders who are truly dedicated to service and caring for others. The power-hungry image of leaders will be replaced with a newer image of inspiring, authentic leaders who love people and want to make an impact that is greater than obtaining six-figure incomes and corner offices.

[The strongest leaders will surround themselves with people who will challenge their every move.]

Won't it be a breath of fresh air to work in an organization that is not loaded with "yes" people who survive day to day by trying to suck up to the boss? The strongest leaders will surround themselves with people who will challenge their every move. They will gain energy and creativity from being challenged. As a result of this new type of group culture, people will feel a sense of belonging and experience higher levels of productivity.

What does this mean for you and your career? It means that you will need to focus on fine-tuning some very important skills. Specifically:

- Communication (with a focus on listening to gain understanding of what is being said and why it is being said);
- Relationship Management/Interpersonal Skills (being open to developing true relationships in the work environment);
- Collaborative Team Development (The emphasis will be placed on creating a team culture where learning from each other is encouraged.

Everyone's input will be valued and respected. Focus on obtaining synergies and efficiencies will be critical.); and

- FLEXIBILITY (Leaders will have to become exceptional at connecting with people from diverse backgrounds. This will require the ability to flex their "normal" behavioral styles in order to understand and extract the best from others.).

[ People don't give tough feedback because it requires some degree of commitment. ]

If you need to make behavioral adjustments, get the help of a professional coach to shorten your learning curve. Refer back to chapter 9, which focuses on coaching and getting help with making lasting behavioral changes. I support using coaches—not because I've become a coach, but because in most of the companies I have worked with it is truly hard to find someone to give you tough, honest feedback. Getting this kind of feedback is critical for your continued development and success. People don't give tough feedback because it requires some degree of commitment. It requires involvement. It's easier to look the other way than to get involved and use energy to help turn someone around.

I had the pleasure of working with a sharp young man who experienced the hard lesson of getting tough feedback. He held the position of a mid-level manager. He had just been moved from the customer service department to the sales department. During his time in the customer service department, he experienced several conflicts with peers and his manager. He was excited to start fresh and to build new relationships. The conflicts that occurred had been resolved and he really felt as though he had put the negative experience behind him.

His performance in the new department was off to a really good start. He was receiving accolades from his manager. He thought that he was on the short list to be promoted. He was shocked when I told him that not only was he probably not on the short list, but he probably wasn't on any list. He couldn't understand what I was saying. I explained to him that it was unrealistic to think that the conflicts that occurred during his time in customer service were just wiped away as though they had never happened. I told him he was dreaming. I challenged him to go back to the people involved with his negative experience and ask for honest feedback. He said he couldn't do it because he hadn't spoken to any of "those" people since leaving the department.

What he eventually found out was that he was viewed as a smart guy who had an ego the size of the world. His ego blinded him from the fact that he had zero people skills. He didn't know how to connect. He was damaged goods. He had been passed on to someone else because the manager whom he reported to in customer service didn't want to invest the time and energy to address his gaps.

I recommended that we use a diagnostic tool to gain a deeper appreciation for his value in the organization, his skill development, and his overall perception. There are several good assessment tools. Just remember that the output is only as good as the honest input. What he learned was that people saw him as brilliant but void of character. He didn't realize how important it was for people to see him as a real person. Had he not been selected to participate in outside coaching, he may not have discovered his gaps until much later on. By then his career may have derailed. When was the last time you completed an assessment on your perception in the organization? If you haven't done it in a while, you might want to. Make sure you select people who are most likely to give you the toughest feedback.

> [ Empowerment is autonomy *with* accountability. ]

### REAL EMPOWERMENT

Collaborative team development will be a great source of motivation for employees. This means that leaders will have to give their employees real empowerment—not lip-service empowerment. When I was in corporate America, the buzzword was "empowering others." No one even understood what empowerment meant. Let me offer this definition: Empowerment is autonomy *with* accountability. I believe this translates into creating an environment where everyone has a really clear understanding of the objective. They truly buy into the objective, and they feel a sense of ownership in the outcome. It also means giving people the space to use their knowledge and talents in a way that promotes the best results. Effective leaders will have to learn to get out of the way and trust that people will do the right thing. Employees will want to be given the benefit of the doubt, instead of having someone standing over their shoulders, walking them through step by step. This is the only way productivity can increase. Employees need the space to be innovative and creative. By releasing their creative energy, new models of business will be discovered.

Real empowerment will be gained through knowledge and information. As a result, organizations will be more forthcoming with information about strategy development, profitability, legal issues or concerns, trends, etc. Information has to be free-flowing throughout the organization. This will prove to be a huge challenge for senior executives, who like holding knowledge because it makes them feel powerful. Closed-door meetings, with the exception of human resource activity, should be outlawed. More often than not, in my experience, closed-door meetings are a distraction that hinders productivity and drains valuable energy.

If employees are really treated and valued as partners, why would it be necessary to withhold information? If you've got the right people doing the right jobs with the right values, what would be the reason not to share information? None, except ego! Let it go. There's no room for it in the new frontier. No one but you cares about your title or your corner office. Get over yourself and get into others. It will be the key to developing yourself and advancing your career. In his book *Side by Side Leadership,* author Denis A. Romig cites research that establishes the benefits of empowering others and creating collaborative teams. He suggests that in companies where workers and leaders abandon old-style, top-down behavior and begin to share leadership, performance improves by 15 percent within six months. He also substantiates the notion that improved productivity results from collaboration. In his assessment, quality, cost control, customer satisfaction, productivity, and profits rose by 20–40 percent within one year in teams where leaders used a side-by-side leadership style.

It makes total sense. And I know this to be true from my own experiences. In my early years as a manager, I completely bought the notion that managers, not the employees, should have the knowledge. It took years before it dawned on me that this was absolutely stupid. I learned this lesson from one of my employees. I was working in the field checking retail outlets with one of the territory sales managers who reported to me. I have never been good at hiding my feelings. My concerns about the business were obviously showing on my face. Vincent, the sales manager, turned to me and said, "You know, you don't have to carry the load all by yourself. That's what the team is for. Let us know what's going on and maybe we would be more willing to help."

I always thought that the leader should be the one with the worries and that worries should not be shared because they would take the focus away from the tasks that needed to be done. That was absolutely wrong! I learned that shared leadership is great. Once I changed my way of thinking, the ideas of the team just started flowing. We would have brainstorming sessions to address particular issues or opportunities. The sum of the team's focus was absolutely fantastic. I began treating my employees as partners, and they, in turn, began to think of me as their partner. We experienced breakthrough performance as a result.

Check yourself in this area. Ask the people you work with if they feel as if they have all the information they need to be successful. Ask them if they feel as if there is a true partnership. If not, take the time to establish partnerships. If this is your first time at engaging in open conversations of this nature, don't be surprised if your feelings are hurt. Sometimes we are better than we think and it takes a little shake-up to keep us on our toes.

## Back to the Basics

The '90s were indeed a decade of discovery. We learned that there is no such thing as job security. We also learned that there is something called information overload. We found out that we don't like being so serious all the time. And we finally gained the wisdom that money doesn't mean total happiness. I personally found out that fun is more valuable than I thought. I also faced the reality that I was missing precious time with my family as a result of my aggressive desire to experience professional success.

Everyone seems to be on the hunt for more time. A lot of information and evidence suggests that, in general, Americans are looking for ways to simplify their lives. Understanding this change is very important for anyone who intends to be a senior leader of an organization. Why? Because in order to create the kind of environment where people are motivated to be productive, you will have to understand what drives their motivation. The next generation of workers wants more than financial compensation. They have a strong desire to experience a "full" life. Work is certainly a part of that full experience, but so is a lot of other stuff. Long gone are the days when a company says, "Jump," and the employee responds, "How high?" This means that there will be a less mobile workforce. It means that companies will have to become a resource in helping their employees deal with all of the realities of life, inclusive of new developments like elder care. Companies will have to respect spiritual rituals that will include things like daily prayer. We can already see this happening. In fact, Ford Motor Company has designated a room in its corporate offices that can be used for naps, prayer, or meditation. Most companies have on-site gyms or exercise classes. Kimberly-Clark has a database that provides sitter service information and elderly care information. Providing these types of resources for employees has proven itself to be successful. A Boston College study, "Measuring the Impact of Workplace Flexibility," found that organizations that built cultures where flexible work arrangements were included found a positive impact on productivity, work quality, and retention.

As a member of a senior leadership team, you will have to help the organization understand that employees who ask for and demand these types of benefits are committed, dedicated employees. It used to be that if an employee talked about anything other than work, he or she was viewed as not being loyal or committed. That kind of thinking will result in the organization losing out on the potential to recruit and retain top talent needed to be successful.

[ The straitlaced, nose-to-the-grindstone model won't work going forward. ]

Another shift that senior leadership will have to embrace is the need for fun in the work environment. Fun? Yes, fun! The straitlaced, nose-to-the-grindstone model won't work going forward. There are numerous studies that suggest that fun is good for business. Southwest Airlines is an organization known for having fun. In an industry that has been hard hit by the declining economy and the events related to September 11, Southwest Airlines remains profitable. Its margins are reportedly the highest in the industry. The CEO has a theory that happy people are productive people. It's a business model that works for them and can work for any other organization willing to create a culture where people enjoy working.

[ Employees want relationships. ]

In addition to fun, employees want relationships. I have talked about leaders connecting with others throughout this book. I believe it is critical to understand how to create relationships. It's important to value relationships. Why do I continue to say this? Think about it. Everything that we as humans do has to do with relationships. Even when we are alone, most of us have an awareness of a relationship with ourselves or with a higher being.

A recent study conducted for Interim Services, Inc., in Ft. Lauderdale, Florida, proves that good relationships do make a difference. The study found that workers who consider their supervisor a friend were more likely to experience high job satisfaction than those who don't (54 percent versus 30 percent), and less likely to look for another job in the next two years (28 percent versus 45 percent).

In the last position I held before leaving the corporate world, I had a team of twenty people. It was an outstanding group of people who were intelligent, energetic, and committed. There was a tremendous amount of change occurring internally and externally for a very long period of time. The net impact was a lot of stress and not very much fun. I didn't realize how much the team was affected until I heard one of them say, "This job just isn't any fun anymore." I knew then that I needed to do something.

I started having weekly debriefing sessions. There was no set agenda for the meeting. It was just time for people to vent. We started eating lunch together as a group, and we played music while we were eating. No business talk was allowed during the lunches. We talked about family, music, religion, and other topics. We started having after-hours get-togethers at the houses of the team members. It was great. Now, traditionally, it wasn't thought to be wise to fraternize with the employees. I didn't agree. This was so important to me that I found a way to overcome that hurdle. It worked. As a result of all these little activities, we were able to reconnect and be a source of support for each other, to better manage the change and the increased performance expectations that had been placed on the team.

## Paying It Forward; Playing It Forward

I want to impress upon you that every generation has a responsibility to pave the way for the generation that follows. Perhaps I'm overly sensitive to this, since my breaking the glass ceiling was very much about sowing seeds so others would reap the rewards. But I know that without the commitment, tenacity, vision, and leadership of those who came before me, I could not have achieved what I was able to achieve. You, too, are a seed sower. The contributions you will make in developing your career can be lasting if you choose to pursue success in a spirit of service.

Knowing what you know now about the changes in the workforce and the strategies and skills needed to develop a successful career, let me ask you a question. What will your contribution be? What mark will you make?

I remember when the concept of seed sowing was introduced to me. I was in college at Loyola University in New

Orleans. I was working my way through school as an administrative assistant for the departments of Religious Studies and Philosophy. Twenty-two professors made up these two departments. I was responsible for normal office duties, but on top of that, I typed manuscript after manuscript, paper after paper. I never had any sense of accomplishment. There was more work than one person could handle. The department actually needed more administrative support, but my request for help fell on deaf ears. Even though the priest I was working for was absolutely a gem, I left that job shortly after graduating from college. And guess what happened. They hired two administrative assistants to replace me. I found out about it through one of the professors with whom I remained in close contact. Once I found out, I immediately called that gem, Father Fagin, to find out how in the world this could have happened. What had changed? Who had changed?

Father Fagin explained to me that after I left, the work began to pile up. The new person insisted that she couldn't do it all. The professors were getting behind in their papers and their manuscripts. "Take comfort in knowing you sowed the seeds," he told me. "What do you mean, I sowed the seeds?" I asked. He responded that in life there are times when we pave the way for things that will happen later on. That message has stuck with me to this very day. In fact, it has become one of my personal principles. If it had not been for that experience, I might not be where I am today.

If you think about the great leaders of this country and this world, perhaps you will come to the same conclusion that I did: All of them were seed sowers. Many of them never even experienced the first harvest of their efforts. But if they had not been willing to pave the way, where would we be? Many of them achieved "firsts." They embraced the unknown.

In fact, they were committed to creating the future. That's what leaders have to be able to do—create the future.

> [ . . . leaders have to be able to . . . create the future. ]

What seeds are you sowing? What daily activities are you involved in that will make a difference for generations to come? Take a few minutes to think about this idea of sowing seeds. What harvest will come as a result of your efforts? If you have not experienced the kind of success that you would like in this area, there's no time like the present. Earlier, when we were identifying what was important to you, I hope you seized the opportunity to truly reflect. In doing this next exercise, I think you will find the link between the difference that you will make on this earth and the beliefs and values that you identified earlier. Use the following lines to write what people would say today, about who you are and what you have contributed during your time thus far on this green earth. If you don't like what you see, choose to change it!

The seeds that I have sowed are:

________________________________________

________________________________________

________________________________________

________________________________________

________________________________________

The new seeds I want to sow are:

________________________________________

________________________________________

____________________________________________________

____________________________________________________

____________________________________________________

I used to start each year with a big kickoff meeting for my team. At that meeting I always read an announcement about the great achievements that we would make during the year. It was read as if they had already happened. That announcement was traditionally read by the president of the company at the following year's sales conference. It was my way of placing a stake in what history would say about my team's accomplishments for the year. It was a great way to make the vision clear . . . to get the buy-in and the commitment. I always included a section entitled "New Innovations." This section was reserved for a new concept or best practice that we would introduce. Many of the ideas and innovative best practices were adopted nationwide.

> [ Don't be afraid to push the envelope and test your limits. ]

Okay, so you know the value of relationships, emotional discipline, and accepting personal responsibility for your own destiny. You will no doubt continue to encounter challenges. You can expect them. Don't be afraid to push the envelope and test your limits. Just as the painter brings a picture to life by using different shades of colors, different types of brushes, and different backgrounds, you, too, can bring to life a fulfilling career if you tap into all your talents, skills, and desires.

You can be part of bridging the gap, and you can experience a very successful career by applying the lessons that you have learned from reading this book. You can be a part of developing yourself as a high performer, developing others as high performers, and creating a positive culture where everyone can flourish and grow. Most people don't get the job they want, let alone the life they want. So seize the moment!

The last thing I want to tell you is to make sure you stop and smell the roses along the way. Celebrate your victories and your successes! Life is indeed a journey full of seasons. Let this be your season to experience success in every facet of your life.

I have included a lot of information in this book. I hope you will take this information and act on it. Knowledge is power, but *only if you put it into action.*

## Points Worth Remembering

- Adopt a personal business principle to stay on top of market developments that can represent an opportunity for the company.
- Keep your focus on getting results and building a diverse team. Help them align their passion with their job.
- True leaders sow seeds that benefit generations to come.
- Celebrate small wins and victories to make the ride far more enjoyable!

# INDEX

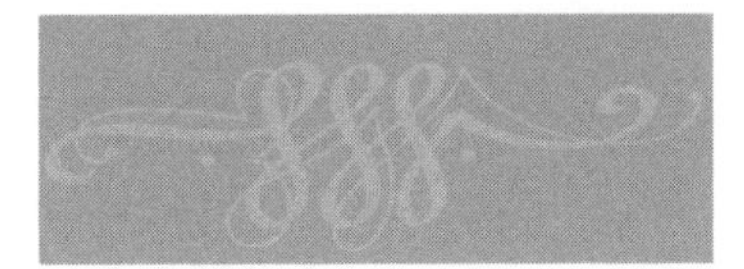

# An Invitation

Here's your opportunity to share your insights, learning, and experiences to help other women achieve their professional goals. I invite you to send your stories (successes and failures) along with the key lessons learned. Send your comments to:

*Her Corner Office*
The Bourgeois Company
3941 Legacy Street, Suite 204, #118B
Plano, TX 75023

## Questions

Ask the coach a question.
Simply log on to www.hybridleader.com and select "Her Corner Office." You'll receive an answer to your question within forty-eight hours. While you're visiting the Web site, take the time to deposit a tip in the best practice sharing corner.

# DEVELOPMENT RESOURCES

| TRUDY'S RESOURCES FOR SUCCESS | REG. PRICE | SPECIAL OFFERS |
|---|---|---|
| THE OPPORTUNITY CALLED CHANGE (CD) | $14.95 | |
| 10 PRINCIPLES OF LEADERSHIP (CD) | $14.95 | |
| ON YOUR WAY TO THE TOP (CD) | $14.95 | |
| MARKETING YOURSELF FOR SUCCESS (CD and Workbooks) Discover the secrets to position yourself for career advancement. | $49.95 | |
| THE TRANSFORMATION LEADERSHIP SERIES SELF STUDY COURSE. This is your opportunity to coach yourself to success! This hands-on down-to-earth personal coaching series is a must for anyone who wants to experience breakthrough success in the 21st century. The lessons imparted from Trudy Bourgeois help you to optimize your strengths, increase your leadership effectiveness, and manage change as an opportunity. THIS IS THE SAME INFORMATION COVERED IN TRUDY'S ANNUAL MONTHLY COACHING PROGRAMS THAT COST MORE THAN $10,000! (Regularly $1,850, now available for a special price of $999) ORDER TODAY AND SAVE $851. | ~~$1,850~~ | $999.00 |

Terms: All Prices shown are in US Dollars, 30-day money back guarantee! Contact us within 30 days of your invoice date if for any reason you're not 100% satisfied with any product you've received from us. Product must be in resellable condition. Your credit card statement will show "Prime Concepts." Appropriate shipping charges will be added to your order.

To order these products please visit our Web site www.hybridleader.com

Tel. 1.866.455.5505 Ph. 972.618.9073 Fax: 972.618.9074 Legacy Dr. Plano TX 75023

**www.HybridLeader.com**

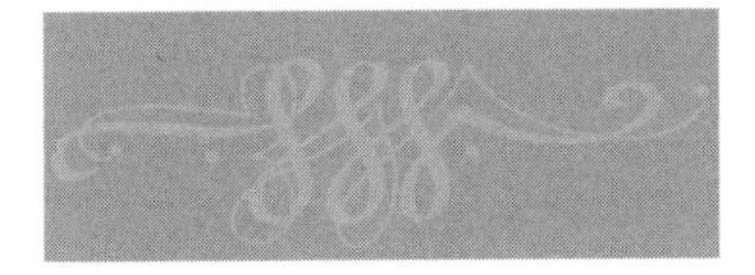

## About the Bourgeois Company

If you enjoyed the information and benefited from the knowledge that Trudy shared in this book, you'll definitely want to add your name to the list to attend her experiential learning summits. These summits are not like traditional workshops. Every program is extremely interactive and is based upon "real-life" business challenges and issues. Topics include:

- Seeds of Leadership for Women
- Her Corner Office: Seven Steps for Powerful Women on Their Way to the Top
- Surviving and Succeeding in Corporate America as a Person of Color
- Targeting Success
- Making a Good Team Great!
- Motivating Your Team to Achieve Great Performance
- Marketing the Brand Called "YOU"

Trudy also speaks to groups across the country. Log on to www.TrudyPresents.com to learn more about The Corporate Transformation Series:

- The Hybrid Leader: Optimizing the Twenty-First-Century Workforce
- Pillars of Excellence: Where the Elite Stand
- Her Corner Office: Seven Steps to Help Women Find a Place and a Voice in Business
- The Opportunity Called "Change"

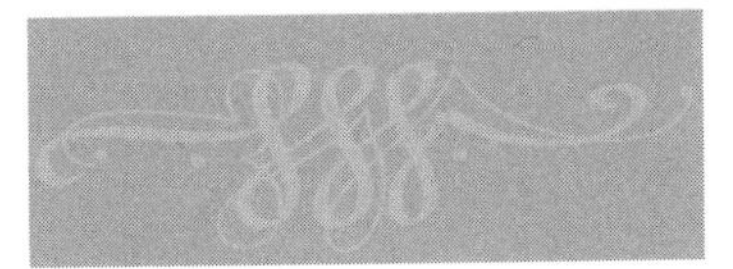

# About the Author

Trudy Bourgeois, a former corporate sales and marketing executive, is the founder and president of The Bourgeois Company. With over twenty years of business experience, Trudy understands what is needed to inspire employees, create workable strategies, and improve employee performance. She has designed and implemented strategies, structures, and marketing programs for Brown and Williamson, and she co-founded their women's leadership forum.

Trudy is a sought-after business coach of both men and women in Fortune 500 companies. She is an expert in developing next-generation leaders and helping individuals take their performances to higher levels.